Chapter 1

What is a freight broker?

A freight broker sells transportation to a shipper, and makes arrangements for the shipment, but does not actually provide the transportation. A broker can be an individual or a company that brings together a shipper that has a need to transport their goods with an authorized motor carrier that wants to provide the service. The broker negotiates the terms of the transaction and manages the shipment from its origin to its destination. The broker is paid a fee for processing the services as an intermediary. The legal name for a freight broker is a "property broker", and the legal definition can be found in the Code of Federal Motor Carrier Regulations. Brokers and their agents provide a valuable service by bringing buyers and sellers together who otherwise couldn't find each other. They use their problem-solving skills to act as transportation consultants and assist in the negotiations regarding the terms of the transportation. Sometimes they take on the role of the company's traffic department, saving them money. They help carriers fill their trucks, help shippers coordinate their transportation services, and locate reliable and authorized motor carriers. The Freight Broker, also called logistics consultants, make a large contribution to our economy, as they keep the transportation industry rolling. Brokers provide efficient and dependable transportation systems, expedited services and just-in-time deliveries, have become a huge strategic asset for corporations, adding significant value to their bottom lines. A freight broker is required to meet the legal requirements outlined by the Federal Motor Carrier Safety Administration (also known as the F.M.C.S.A., a division of the Department of Transportation/D.O.T.).

Freight Forwarder

A freight broker is sometimes confused with a freight forwarder. They are both "wholesalers" of transportation services. However, a licensed freight broker does not declare an interest in the cargo, whereas a licensed freight forwarder is required to be insured, and DOES take possession of the freight. The freight forwarder usually handles freight from port of export to overseas port of import, whereas the freight broker normally arranges for truckload freight that is transported over the road. A freight forwarder is licensed by the Federal Maritime Commission, and a freight broker is licensed by the Federal Motor Carrier Safety Administration.

What are the Requirements to be a Freight (Property) Broker?
If you want to become a Freight Broker, you are required to meet the legal requirements outlined by the Federal Motor Carrier Safety Administration. These requirements are:
1. BROKER **AUTHORITY** The authority to operate as a licensed freight broker is required and administered by the FMCSA.*Freight Brokers must be registered with the FMCSA by filing a Form OP-1 or go to https://www.fmcsa.dot.gov/registration. *Brokers are required to possess a Motor Carrier Number, also called a (MC#). A broker's MC Number will always be followed by a "B". Note: *There are companies that will file your broker's authority paperwork for a fee, or you can file for it yourself.

2. SURETY BOND A surety bond is a legal document that gives evidence that a broker has the financial responsibility to compensate the motor carrier for contracted services. Normally, financial statements are provided to an insurance company that issues the bond in the name of the broker. The FMCSA requires the bond for a freight broker to be $75,000 (FMCSA Regulation #387.307). The FMCSA form for this is either form BMC-84 for a surety bond, or it can be in the form of a $75,000 trust fund agreement with a financial institution, which is form BMC-85. The FMCSA will not issue a freight (property) broker license until a surety bond or trust fund is in effect.

3. PROCESS AGENTS A process agent is a legal representative upon whom court papers may be served in any proceeding brought against a broker, motor carrier, or freight forwarder. *The FMCSA also requires brokers to secure process agents in each state in which they are to conduct business, which will be in all of the contiguous 48 states. According to the FMCSA, those with a MC# shall make a designation for each state in which they are authorized to operate, and for each state traversed during the operation. Brokers are required to list process agents in each state in which they have an office and in each state in which they write contracts (again, the 48 states). The FMCSA form for this is the BOC-3 form. You do not have to locate legal agents for yourself. Many commercial firms will arrange process agents in any state for a fee. You can find a list of companies that provide this service on the FMCSA website at www.fmcsa.dot.gov/factsfigs/licensing/agents.htm.

Freight Broker Agent

A freight broker agent typically secures the customer as well as the carrier as part of his or her job. As a freight broker agent, the contract with the broker is typically set up where there is a commission split on the gross profit margin between you and the broker. The amount of your commission and your responsibilities with the broker will be dependent on the terms of your individual broker/agent agreement and contract. There are no set or standard contracts in this industry. In general, the current average trend in the marketplace for the majority of freight brokers is around a 40 to 50% split on the gross profit of each load – in other words, on a 50% split, 50% of the profit on the shipment goes to the agent and 50% goes to the broker. This trend in the last few years has been in the agent's favor, whereas 3 to 5 years ago the trend was closer to 30% for the agent and 70% for the broker. Remember, to be a freight broker agent, an individual is not required to obtain federal licensing or put up a bond, or obtain process agents, as a broker is required to do. The basic requirements are a place to work (most work out of home offices), a computer with high speed internet, and a business email address, a phone with unlimited incoming and outgoing long distance service, a fax machine, discipline, and the motivation to work. What else is required to be a freight broker agent? First, you must have a contract with a licensed and bonded freight broker or brokerage firm, under whose authority you will conduct business. Second, you need training – which is why you're reading this! You need to know how to begin your marketing, where to find shippers and how to develop your client database, how to find authorized and dependable motor carriers, how to determine market rates in a fast-changing industry sector based on supply and demand. You need to be able to work on a commission basis, unless you plan to start out in an hourly dispatcher position first, since the trend is that over 90% of broker-agent agreements are set up this way. Understand that this is a relationship business. It takes time at the beginning to build up your client database and income. You need to be prepared for this initial gap period, either with cash reserves or another source of income. It is important, though, for someone to be able to answer your phones and help clients during business hours. If you are trying out this business while you maintain a second job, you should consider job sharing with another agent who also needs a flexible schedule. Or you can work out an agreement with your broker. This industry is an "early bird catches the worm" business, and is fast paced- so if you are unavailable, you will most likely lose the business. If you aren't available to help a shipper in need, he will call another broker or agent, and you will have missed the opportunity. For a new individual starting out, making 40-50 contact calls per day, it can take an average of 3 to 6 months to start building up your client database. This is the hardest part – the initial "breaking the ice" period, when you are building relationships and building up trust with potential clients. The good news is that once you begin securing clients, it is a residual business, and doesn't require a lot of clients to make a good income. As long as you continue to service your clients well, they normally continue shipping month after month and year after year – and over time, as you continue securing more clients, your revenue snowballs. Freight brokering is a fast-paced industry that involves a rapidly changing commodity. The introduction of the "just-in-time" freight management concept in the last several years is rapidly spreading in our current business climate. The industry itself is highly fragmented, which also boosts the need for freight brokers and agents. The truckload sector is largely privately owned, with some exceptions of the top publicly owned companies. Of the 50,000 smaller truckload carriers, it is estimated that 95% have annual revenues of less than $1 million. Most of these smaller carriers do not have the ability to have a sales team on their staff. This is where the need for brokers and agents comes in. The number of independent smaller motor carriers is continuing to grow at a rapid pace, with approximately 150 new motor carrier license applications submitted to the FMCSA daily. Even with this rapid growth in the number of small motor carriers, current supply, or capacity of trucks, is still tight due to the tight supply of qualified drivers, so freight rates have skyrocketed. More and more corporations of all sizes, watching their freight expenditures skyrocket, are continuing to turn to logistics consultants, such as freight brokers and agents, for help. Information technology and the software industry, especially those with live data and web-based applications, are in the midst of a revolution. Recent exponential growth of e-businesses has caused an explosion in the amounts and types of information available at one's fingertips. The challenge for today's businesses is "information integration" – to be able to reach out across the internet, to process, combine and extract information from the vast amounts available, and to transform it into "information assets". "Information assets" can be applied to daily business to achieve increased business opportunities. Brokers and agents that can access information and apply this data will be in the strongest position to grow in the market. The growth of the internet has leveled the playing field in many respects, so that small companies can now compete in a much larger market, alongside the industry giants.

What is double brokering and is it legal?

Double brokering is when a broker (or an agent of the broker) tenders a shipment to another broker, instead of to a carrier. This is illegal. You can go to jail. Why? Because even in the very first section of the FMCSA's legal definition of a broker (Sec. 371.2 (a)), it states that a broker arranges the transportation of property by an AUTHORIZED MOTOR CARRIER. An authorized motor carrier is authorized to transport the shipment and is legally bound to it – another broker is not. Brokerage services can be performed "on behalf of a motor carrier, a consignor, the shipper, or consignee (receiver)", not on behalf of another broker. In addition, one of the records that you are required to keep as a broker is the "date of payment to the carrier" (Sec. 371.3) there would not be a transaction if the load was double brokered, as the payment would be made to the other broker. As an ethical broker, you must check to make sure that your carrier is authorized with a motor carrier license and that the carrier has current cargo insurance coverage to protect your shipper. If you were to give the load to another broker, obviously he would have neither of the above requirements. Besides being illegal, you would also be negligent to your shipper, who has trusted you to tender their load legally, and make sure that it is insured. You would have no control over whether the other broker even used a legal carrier. You would have misrepresented yourself to your client by implying that you were going to tender the client's load to a reputable carrier. If an insurance claim were to occur, there very likely might be no coverage, and you could be held for negligence. You would also surely lose your client over your business practices. §371.13 accounting: Each broker who engages in any other business shall maintain accounts so that the revenues and expenses relating to the brokerage portion of its business are segregated from its other activities. Expenses that are common shall be allocated on an equitable basis; however, the broker must be prepared to explain the basis for the allocation. [45FR 68943, Oct. 17, 1980]

Form OP-1 (Revised: 09/27/2013)　　　　　　　　　　　　　　　　　　　　　　OMB No. 2126-0016　Expiration Date: 10/31/2015

U.S. Department of Transportation
Federal Motor Carrier Safety Administration

FORM OP-1　APPLICATION FOR MOTOR PROPERTY CARRIER AND BROKER AUTHORITY

This application is for all businesses requesting Operating Authority as a motor carrier, broker, and/or U.S.-based enterprise carrier of property or household goods.

FOR FMCSA USE ONLY	
Docket No. MC	Fee No.
Filed	CC Approval No.

SECTION I — Applicant Information

1. Do you now have authority from or an application being processed by the FMCSA, FHWA, OMCS, or ICC? ◯ Yes ◯ No	If yes, identify the MC/FF Number (or lead docket number):

2. LEGAL BUSINESS NAME	3. DOING BUSINESS AS NAME (If different from Legal Business Name)

PRINCIPAL ADDRESS (PRINCIPAL PLACE OF BUSINESS)

4. STREET NAME AND NUMBER (No P.O. Box)	5. CITY	6. STATE	7. ZIP CODE	8. TELEPHONE NUMBER	9. FAX NUMBER

MAILING ADDRESS (If different from Principal Address above)

10. STREET NAME AND NUMBER	11. CITY	12. STATE	13. ZIP CODE	14. TELEPHONE NUMBER	15. FAX NUMBER

REPRESENTATIVE (person who can respond to inquiries)

16. NAME	17. TITLE, POSITION, OR RELATIONSHIP TO APPLICANT

18. STREET NAME AND NUMBER	19. CITY	20. STATE	21. ZIP CODE	22. TELEPHONE NUMBER	23. FAX NUMBER

24. USDOT NUMBER (If available; if not, see instructions)

FORM OF BUSINESS (select only one)

◯ 25. CORPORATION　　STATE OF INCORPORATION _____

◯ 26. SOLE PROPRIETORSHIP　LEGAL NAME OF OWNER _____

◯ 27. PARTNERSHIP　　LEGAL NAME OF EACH PARTNER _____

SECTION II — Type of Operating Authority (select at least one)

28. Check box(es) for each type of Operating Authority requested. You must submit a filing fee of $300.00 for each box checked.

☐ Motor Common Carrier of Property (except Household Goods)　　☐ Broker of Property (except Household Goods)

☐ Motor Contract Carrier of Property (except Household Goods)　　☐ Broker of Household Goods

☐ Motor Common Carrier of Household Goods　　☐ United States-based Enterprise Carrier of International Cargo (except Household Goods)

☐ Motor Contract Carrier of Household Goods　　☐ United States-based Enterprise Carrier of International Household Goods

SECTION III — Insurance Information (Applicants that will operate commercial motor vehicles must complete this section.)

29. The dollar amounts in parentheses represent the minimum amount of bodily injury and property damage (liability) insurance coverage you must maintain and have on file with the FMCSA. (Refer to the instructions for information about cargo insurance requirements for motor common carriers and United States-based enterprise carriers, and surety bond/trust fund agreement filings for brokers.)

Applicant will operate one or more vehicle(s) having a gross vehicle weight rating (GVWR) of 10,000 pounds or more to transport:

☐ Non-hazardous commodities ($750,000)

☐ Hazardous materials referenced in FMCSA's insurance regulations at 49 CFR 387.9 ($1,000,000)

☐ Hazardous materials referenced in FMCSA's insurance regulations at 49 CFR 387.9 ($5,000,000)

Applicant will operate only vehicles having gross vehicle weight ratings (GVWR) under 10,000 pounds to transport:

☐ Any quantity of Division 1.1, 1.2, or 1.3 material; any quantity of Division 2.3, Hazard Zone A, or Division 6.1, Packing Group I, Hazard Zone A material; or highway route controlled quantities of a Class 7 material as defined in 49 CFR 173.403 ($5,000,000)

☐ Commodities other than those listed above ($300,000)

Chapter
2

Why Become A Broker Agent?

You may be asking yourself, why should you become a broker agent? Becoming a broker agent is a rewarding job. This is because of the large amount of freedom involved – you get to be your own boss! In this career you may choose to work either from home or in the office, and the financial rewards are incredibly beneficial. Not only that, but you will also be awarded personally by helping others. Listen there are certain characteristics that will help you be successful as a freight broker or agent. Number one, you have to be patient. You have to be focused, and you have to be diligent. You have to be patient, especially during the early start-up phase of your broker agency. You have to be focused and diligent during this time, not only patient. We're not talking about just making a sale, we're talking about making a customer - and you're usually taking a customer away from somebody. It takes about eight to nine touches for a customer to make a change. This includes phone calls, emails, rate quotes, personalized cards, and, the most important, a personal visit. You know, in every phone call you make, your ultimate goal should be to get in front of your customer. If you've done that, you're about 50% ahead of the game. Basically you need to be self-motivated to do anything. If you can punch a clock for somebody else, you can certainly punch a clock for yourself. You know, business is like an organism, it's got to grow. Your job is to take away whatever it is that's keeping your business from growing, and for most businesses it's because they don't prospect. You've got to be disciplined enough to set your prospecting goals, and time to prospect.

Four Cornerstones

The four cornerstones of the industry include the consignor, which is the shipper, the broker, the motor carrier and the consignee, or the receiver. The shipper gives the broker the load. The broker finds a truck, and gives the truck the load. The truck then delivers to the consignee. This visual emphasizes the importance of being more than an order taker. You have to offer more than the carrier, or using a broker is pointless. A shipper could give the load directly to the carrier and cut out the broker. However, the shipper does not have access to the tools the broker has to find carriers; so many shippers only use brokers. If you plan on being a broker you must gain the trust of the shipper, the carrier and the consignee.

Benefits and Opportunities

As a freight broker or as an agent for a broker, it is important for you to understand the benefits and opportunities that you can offer to your potential clients. It is significant to understand exactly what you are marketing and selling, before you can sell it. As a broker or an agent, you are a non-asset based service company. What kind of service will you offer? What benefits and opportunities are you furnishing your shipper? Let's look at an actual letter from a customer. We asked a corporate traffic manager for a large shipper to answer this question for us: From a customer's point of view, what do you look for in a freight broker? Here is the answer:

HONESTY. It is important to be up front and honest with your customer, especially in the critical situations. (Examples are truck delays, damage or stolen goods, accidents and trucks that do not show up.)

DEPENDABILITY. Your customer is looking for someone dependable that will be available for them when they call in need of freight rates, looking for a last minute truck, or when they need you to pull a rabbit out of your hat.

TEAM WORK. You want to be on your customer's team to help get their job done efficiently and effectively. You are working as an extension of their office. (Examples are making delivery appointments, dispatching, helping with freight claims, updating status reports.)

RATES AND SERVICE. Every customer would love to save money if possible but service is more important. The key is getting shipments to the destination on time. Sometimes the customer is willing to pay a little extra for better service.

COMMUNICATION. Communication is very important. Always communicate with your customer. Emails are great for rate confirmations and status reports. Phone calls are more personal. They show the customer you are taking a little extra effort to keep in touch, especially during a crisis situation.

Account Manager Responsibilities

It is your responsibility as an account manager for your client, to ask questions. Listen closely; write down what they say. Find out what they are looking for in a freight broker or agent – and provide those services! Help them do their job. You need to be creative in order to meet the specific needs of your individual clients. You may even think of some things to help them that they haven't even thought of. After all, you are a consultant. Your objective is to be there to consult with them and help them achieve the specific transportation goals of their company.

Traits of a Successful Broker/Agent

What should a carrier look for when choosing a broker agent? First make sure that the broker is licensed by the FMCSA. A carrier should choose a broker based on the proper authority and license. Carriers will typically run a credit check on the broker. Freight brokers should be financially sound. Carriers expect to be paid on time no matter what. Even if the shipper does not pay the broker on time, the broker still needs to pay the carrier on time. The historical norm is for a carrier's bill to be due net 30 from the receipt of the invoice and original proof of delivery, which is the signed bill of lading. To avoid unwanted surprises and problems, brokers/agents must communicate constantly with their carriers. Giving instructions over the phone is never enough. Look for thorough brokers/agents who communicate in writing when instructing carriers. Ask brokers how they match carriers to available loads. How do they confirm that loads were picked up and delivered as promised? Remember communication is the key in this business, and the only thing that the broker or agent can control.

Relationships

If you're a broker or a carrier, you should always get everything in writing. There needs to be a broker- carrier contract that explains the terms and conditions of your agreement, to help avoid misunderstandings. Trust and relationships are built over time. Remember the carrier relationship should be regarded as just as important to the broker as the shipper/client relationship. The carrier is doing the job/providing the service. The broker or agent needs to treat the carrier with the same amount of respect that he expects to receive from the carrier. The broker/agent and the carrier must build mutual credibility with each other, just as the broker/agent is building credibility with the shipper client. This relationship is critical for your success in this industry. It is much better if a carrier can do business with the same broker on a regular basis. This is much better than the broker/agent posting their loads every time and using a different carrier on each load. Remember this all starts with mutual respect. The carrier should be offered a fair price and an honest company to do business with.

Success
What must a broker/agent do to be successful? Build strong relationships with qualified shippers and qualified motor carriers. Know how to determine and negotiate rates. Pay close attention to details. Watch cash flow and profit margins and set and achieve goals - it takes a plan.

Market Trends
It is imperative that you become and stay aware of what is going on in the marketplace. Let's look at some of the trends. Due to the current economic conditions and uncertainties, oil prices are skyrocketing and continue to fluctuate today. Operating costs also rose causing a large number of the smaller carriers to be forced out of business. Many of the larger carriers have had to increase their rates substantially. A few years ago, overall freight rates rose approximately 40%.

Supply and Demand
Truck supply, also called truck capacity, meets demand at some point. Supply and demand swings in both directions, and changes on a regular basis. Right now for the first time in a long time, there is significantly more freight than available trucks. Since capacity is tight, trucks can command higher rates, and customers are willing to pay them. In almost every state, there is more freight than trucks. The exceptions are geographic areas that have high populations but not a lot of manufacturing facilities, like Maine, New York, and Florida.

Security

In addition, another trend is that more and more shipments that formerly would have shipped by air are now being put on trucks, since 9-11 brought tightened air regulations, and a heightened security was implemented. Because of this, since air freight is usually time sensitive freight, this increased the need for critical ground services that can deliver quickly - often called just in time delivery. A broker or agent can assign a shipment to a truck with a 2 driver team, and the shipment can deliver to most destinations in the U.S. almost as quickly as if it had been shipped via air freight. And critical care time and expedited ground freight can command much higher prices, especially if it has to have a guaranteed delivery time.

Consolidating Shipments

Still another trend is that many fortune 100 companies, instead of shipping multitudes of smaller, less than truckload (LTL) shipments, are starting to move toward sending their smaller shipments into regional distribution centers, and then consolidating their LTL shipments into truckload (TL) shipments that will then be sent cross-country as TL freight. This offers them substantial cost savings and reduces damages. This is because LTL shipments are loaded and reloaded many times, whereas TL freight is typically only loaded once and then off-loaded, lowering the risk of damages. Many brokers and agents help them facilitate this process. This process also has increased the need for truckload services. Others are moving more freight by inter-modal or rail due to fuel prices. This is typically more common for shipments that are not time sensitive. To do an inter-modal project, as a broker or agent, you would need to team up with one of the larger inter-modal companies in the industry because railroads normally won't work directly with smaller brokerage firms or carriers – only the larger rail players.

Seasonal Market Trends

There are also often seasonal market trends within the transportation industry, which raise or lower carrier rates as well as determine what commodities are hot at certain times. They can determine where carriers are migrating to geographically. Some examples of seasonal trends are Christmas trees, flowers at Mother's Day, and seasonal produce such as certain fruits and potatoes, which all have a high volume of shipping from certain areas for a short period of time. As seasonal market trends open up, carriers tend to migrate to those areas of heavy shipping. Because these seasonal loads only last for a short period of time, there is an urgency to get the product to market. The carriers will command a higher rate for these loads. This can also create a shortage of trucks in other geographical regions, again, commanding a higher rate.

Short Term Trends
Weather also plays a part in geographical market trends, especially for the short term. As winter descends on the northern part of the United States, many carriers choose not to haul loads into traditionally bad snow belt areas. Disasters will affect short-term trends of supply and demand. For example, Hurricane Katrina had a big impact on the transportation industry, in that so many carriers were needed by the federal government to bring in food, water and supplies, that a huge deficit in available carriers was created. This along with the astronomical gas prices blamed on Katrina created a huge surplus of freight that needed to be moved, causing exceptionally high rates. The trend continued for many months in the aftermath of Katrina.

Learning Market Trends
It is difficult to learn market trends other than what time and experience as a broker/agent can give you. If you are diligent and resourceful, you can speed up the process by talking to carriers and asking them what type of freight they are moving, what lanes they are running, and what the hot commodity is right now. You can also talk to other broker/agents and research the internet. There are logistics and trucking trade magazines and web sites that will give you this type of information if you keep up with their news. Most importantly, watch, ask and learn as you build your brokerage.

Market Niches and the Broker Agent
A niche market is a focused and targeted portion of a market. Often, you may find that brokerages specialize in or cater to a specific need within their general market or customer base. This is especially true for more established brokerages. Many times these niches occur

naturally and come about slowly. Over time, a broker will become more knowledgeable in one particular area of the transportation industry. This may be completely unintentional and arise out of a need to satisfy a specific shipper's special requirements. In the process of meeting these requirements, the broker gains an overt knowledge of certain requirements and uses that knowledge to gain additional shippers with the same needs. This gives the broker a definitive edge over the brokers whose knowledge is limited in the special requirements of that type of shipper. At other times, a new broker may choose to learn these needs deliberately in the hopes of increasing sales by targeting that particular market, utilizing his new found knowledge.

Geographic and Expedited Niches
However a niche market or specialization is derived at, competition is generally more limited. However, the potential rewards can appear unlimited. Some of the more typical niche markets include:
1. Geographical Niches: Sometimes for a new broker or agent, the easiest target market to focus on is your own geographical area- especially if you are located in an area with a lot of manufacturers, a port area, or an unusually heavy shipping area. You can use a shipper's guide, such as the manufacturer's guide, and utilize the geographic section, to target market by city, starting with your own city, or ones that are close by. If you focus within a tight geographic area, you can develop the area more quickly. You will get to know the ins and outs of that area's shipping activities and contacts.

2. Expedited Freight: There is always a shipper somewhere who is running late on a shipment, or a customer that has to have a shipment delivered the quickest way possible so that production is not slowed down and revenue is not lost. Because of situations like these, there are brokers and agents who specialize in expedited freight. They have learned, often through trial and error, how to find trucks quickly and most importantly how to move them quickly. This is often done through team drivers who take turns driving non-stop until the load is delivered and using preferred carriers who they know will not deviate from the job at hand. These brokers may also target air freight forwarders who have shipments delayed due to bad weather, missed flights or stepped up security measures. In these

situations, it is often quicker to move the load by ground to its desired destination.

Sector Marketing and Equipment Specialization
3. Sector Marketing: Some brokers or agents decide on a certain sector that they enjoy dealing with, and decide to focus on that specific sector. Some examples could be the retail sector, the food industry sector, or electronics sector. If you decide to focus on a specific sector, you should strive to become the expert on the shipping needs for that sector.

4. Equipment Specialization: Another idea for a niche market is to specialize on a certain type of van. For example, there are many companies that ship substances in the form of chemicals or food grade liquid. These liquid substances have to be shipped by tankers. The number of tanker carriers is relatively small when compared to the number of dry van or refrigerated van carriers. Building a good preferred carrier list for tanker companies is essential when dealing with shippers who use them. Gaining knowledge of the different type of tankers available, as well as health and safety issues, is imperative when targeting this niche market. Some other examples of equipment types that you could specialize in are refrigerated vans or flatbeds.

Commodity Specialization
5. Commodity Specialization: One agent came across specializing in the commodity of foam, just because it happened to be her first major client's product. She found that it was an easy product to deal with because of low damages. She was able to get her foot in the door easier with other foam companies, because she let them know that she was already familiar with the shipping of foam products. Before long, she was the foam expert. Another broker started specializing in shipping a certain type of machinery because he came up with a shipping solution for a client. In the past, they always had to ship their machinery on very specialized expensive equipment. He found a way to bend one part of the machine down, and ship the equipment on a regular van, saving the company thousands and thousands of dollars. It soon became a natural niche for him, because he was able to translate this savings to many companies around the

country that shipped this same type of machinery. Still a third agent, decided to choose produce as his niche. Many brokers and agents won't deal with produce – because in produce, there are often games played between the shipper and the consignee, with the carrier stuck in the middle – and it can cause a lot of delay and headaches. For example, a shipper may be selling a load of grapes and shipping them from California to El Paso. When they arrive in El Paso, the consignee calls the shipper and says that the grapes don't look so good – that a lot of them look mashed. He doesn't know if he wants them, and he definitely doesn't want to pay full price for them. The shipper can't view the product, now that it is in El Paso, but one thing that he does know is that he doesn't want to pay to have the grapes shipped back to California; they would all be spoiled by then. So now, the shipper and the consignee start over with their price negotiations, and all the while, the trucker is caught in the middle, because he has to sit and wait, and he can't unload the product. Because of true stories such as this, many brokers don't even want to handle produce. But a broker agent with a specialization in produce, knows all the produce games well, and he has come up with some solutions. So he is up to the challenge. He was able to come up with some creative solutions for the frustrations that go along with produce – and he figured out how to make it a profitable niche for him.

Hazardous Materials

6. Hazardous materials are extremely dangerous, and require special knowledge in handling and transporting as well as additional licenses and insurance. As one could guess, due to the nature of the materials being shipped and the high risk and liability involved, the number of brokers and carriers that are able to move these materials is relatively small, so they can command much higher rates. There are many examples of niche markets such as flatbed haulers, permitted heavy haul, refrigerated products such as ice cream, – the list could go on and on. It may be that you create your own niche that has never been developed before. Pick one and learn all that you can about it, or let one occur naturally. Either way, a niche market can bring higher revenues to a broker or an agent, rather than just moving any type of freight that is available.

Know Your Competition

Use your search engine to look up freight broker and trucking companies. Read their web sites and get any useful information that you can from the site. Useful information may include: company size, number of trucks, number of agents, years in business, niche markets or specialties, what lanes they run, how many offices they have and where, and if they are both a carrier and a broker. Sometimes they list the different loads that they have available daily. This will give you an idea of their size and how many loads that they move in a day. The site may also include a quote page in which brokers have been known to ask for a quote on a particular lane to get price comparisons. Be prepared though, if you request a rate quote, you may just get a phone call.

Do Your Research

Ask your prospects and your established customers when you call on them who they use or have used in the past. Find out what they liked and disliked about that broker or carrier and how their rates compare. Ask about their service and how they handled problems and if they still use that broker, why or why not. Ask your carriers about the other brokers that they use. Who are the big broker players in the industry and how do they compare to the smaller brokers? Ask who the carriers prefer to haul for and why. Find out who pays a higher rate and who pays on time. Network within the industry. Hire seasoned agents who have been in the business for several years. They are a wealth of knowledge. They may have worked for several brokers and can tell you many stories about the competition as well as the carriers. Don't be afraid to ask a prospect who they currently use, especially if they tell you that they are satisfied with their current broker or carrier. Tell them that is great - that you are new to the business, and would like to ask them why they like that broker, and what they would look for in a new broker if they needed to find another one. Knowing your competition is essential. As you become aware of who your main competitors are with your prospects and clients, and how they run their operations, it will influence your rate quotes, and your rate quotes will sometimes depend on your current competition for that particular project. Extra services that you provide may be determined by your competition, and even the ability to work with a particular shipper may be determined by your competition. In this business as in any other sales business, the top sales people always take the extra time and effort to research the competition. A good general always takes the time to know his enemy.

Networking
Networking is essential as a freight broker or agent. Networking is simply building alliances with companies who have complementary services, attending events with potential customers and vendors, and meeting with other small business owners. Join your local chamber of commerce, trade associations and professional clubs. As a broker or agent, you may work much of the time by yourself. Networking gives you the opportunity to talk with others, exchange ideas and talk through issues that may have come up with others that have already worked it out. In our technologically advanced society having a network of others who are working on a similar computer system is priceless. Dynamic networking will also help keep you motivated to succeed. One source for networking is trade shows. There are transportation and logistics trade shows that you can attend, where you can meet new vendors, see what's new in the industry, and, while you are there, you can check up on what your competitors are doing. You can network with carriers at trucking trade shows, and align yourself with companies that are selling complementary products and services. A great type of trade show to attend is a show that your prospective clients would attend – such as a trade show for manufacturers, or a show for the niche market that you have chosen, such as a trade show for food companies. Or a trade show specifically held in an industry sector that you are either already doing business in or want to pursue. The best one would be a show that has no other transportation service companies; this would be a good trade show to purchase a booth to advertise your service, network as much as possible, and hand out your business cards and advertising fliers or brochures. Network with people and companies that can educate and coach you in the brokering industry or in sales. Continually adding to your knowledge in the field would add value to your business as a consultant. Anytime you can take a class and network with educators in your industry, you are ahead of the game. You can also take classes and network with sales consultants and

coaches. For example, you could take a class in the skill of negotiating, which is a skill you can always improve on, and will help improve your bottom line as a broker/agent.

Know Your Client

When you go out to a client's office, your goal should be to network and get to know everyone that you can in their organization. Meet the receptionist, or whoever you come across and get to know them on a person basis, even by name. Getting person is one of the fastest ways to break down walls, and get to know people. Network to find out the internal decision-making process in the company, and the chain of command. Of course, your primary contact that you are calling on is the decision-maker that is routing the truckload or large shipments. However, you will want to work to get to know their boss, their boss's boss, their assistants, and the company owner. They may have a traffic manager, but someone else, above or below them, may really be calling the day-to-day shots. Ask who makes the decisions about shipping. Get their name, email address and extension. Get to know their company philosophies, their goals, and where individual employees are headed. Research them on the internet. Get creative. Discuss with them about their shipping issues, or just get to know them. If their traffic manager gets transferred to another department or leaves the company, you will be glad that you have built up a relationship with the next person in line that takes their place. And you know the company really likes you when you finally get invited to the company event like a holiday party or an appreciation party for their vendors! Of course, all of this is a process; building up trust and relationships takes time and effort.

Sales

There is one aspect of the job that most people have mixed feelings about. In order to build your client list, you have to participate in sales activities. Like everything else there are things that people like and things that they don't like. They like the money that can be made. They like the relationships they build and the feeling of trust that develops as the relationship grows. And, they enjoy the ability to be in control of their schedule, especially the part about setting their own hours. They don't like prospecting. Most people have a certain hesitation about calling strangers. They fear the rejection they might experience when trying to contact a new prospect. Along with rejection comes a feeling that they may be shown a lack of respect by some of the people. However, if you want to be successful as a broker/agent, you have to call prospects. You have to sell. CALL CALL CALL

Roles and Tasks

One of the reasons people have these reservations is that they see selling as a role they must assume. But it is actually just a task. The role you are assuming in this profession is that of a consultant. Your purpose is to build a relationship with the potential client in order to help them run their business better by providing great service and information. The consultant's role requires you to understand your purpose in relationship to your customer. What do you provide your customer that they cannot do for themselves? How do your services differ from others? How do your values tell the customer that you are reliable and trustworthy? These are the things you must be able to communicate to them. This is your role in the customer's business. Sales are a task that must be successfully carried out to begin the relationship. What you need to learn to be able to sell as a broker/agent is really quite simple. It only takes some discipline, commitment, time, and work.

Trust & Relationships

There are four reasons people don't buy from you – they don't know and trust you, no need for your service, no hurry, or no want. The bottom line is that you need to build up trust. The faster you build up trust with someone, the more you're going to learn about the other three. And the way you build up trust with people is you do what you say you're going to do, when you say you're going to do it, and you don't quit on them. If you say you're going to call them back next week, you call them back next week. They're not going to give you the business on the first call, and if it's all about rates, then this is not a good prospect for you - because as soon as the rate goes up, the relationship goes away. This is very important: You need to be proactive, take initiative and go the extra mile. Time is worth more than money. Don't give them a reason of why they should use you. Every prospect is asking the same question: What's in it for me?

Find out what's in it for them, help them meet their goals, whether it's the carrier or the shipper, and you'll be successful. Remember, before they're going to tell you the truth about what their goals really are, you're going to have to build up trust with them. Once the trust is built up and you have the relationship built up, then they'll invite you into the company. It's not really your account unless you're invited to the office parties and they know your kids by name. Relationships are the key.

Five Steps to Qualify Potential Customers
There are five steps in the process of qualifying potential customers.

Step 1 is the selection of prospects; those people who you believe will be interested in your services.

Step 2 requires that you call each of these prospects on the phone, at least 50 a day.

Step 3 demands that you establish your credibility. This is the beginning step. Establishing your credibility in the eyes of your customer is an on-going process from this point forward.

Step 4 is to develop a customer profile. Make a form that will provide you with key pieces of information that you need. However, the information is not the only things you will need to learn about your customers. You have to be alert for the information that will help provide outstanding service, and will allow you to move the relationship forward.

Step 5 necessitates that you discover and confirm what the customer needs in terms of service from you. Only when you have moved to this point in the relationship will you be able to turn the prospect into a customer.

Selecting Prospects
An excellent source of manufacturing companies is the Manufacturer's Register. You need to obtain a copy for the area that

you plan to ship from. From the book, you should choose 50 businesses to call. This is your first day's call list. The companies you choose should be chosen based on how well they fit the established criteria. You can also use sites like manta.com, referenceusa.com, jigsaw.com bizjournals.com, mcraebluebook.com and find articles.com.

Phone Calls

Step two is to make the phone calls, all fifty of them. Develop the habit of writing down a daily call schedule. It doesn't have to be all at one time. It may be easier for you and you schedule if you try a few times throughout the day. But make sure that what's important is to make ALL the calls. There are two types of calls that you will be making: Initial Contact Calls and Daily Calls. Initial contact calls are made to establish contact and to qualify prospects. Daily calls are made to service customers that you have already contact. When you begin, most of your calls will be initial contacts. As you qualify prospects, the ratio of daily calls to initial calls will increase. You should keep the total number of calls at a minimum of 50 until you have a customer base that makes it impossible to make that number of calls.

The Numbers Game

Let's talk about a numbers game in sales. Now I don't care what you're selling, yes and no pays the same. Think about that for a minute. If I gave you 50 prospects to call, and you called those 50 prospects every day - I can't guarantee you, - we would get an opportunity to move a load, and that the average load would be around $500. So, that makes each call worth about $10. If I sat down there behind you, and I put a $10 every time you made a call, if I put that on the table for you to pick up and put in your pocket - whether you got a voice mail, whether you got a yes, or whether you got a no, or call me back tomorrow - I guarantee you'd make those fifty calls before 10 every day. That's what this is all about. You've got to prospect every day, you've got to make the calls, and that's really about what it works out to be; $10 a call.

Call Reluctance

Many new Freight Brokers are reluctant to make phone calls to prospective customers. There are a few people who can make the calls without any hesitation. However, most will feel anxious about making the call. Why? You fear the worse will happen, that you will be rejected because you did something wrong! You disturbed them when you shouldn't. You'll sound like a telemarketer. You'll start the call wrong. You'll end the call wrong. You won't ask enough questions. You won't ask the right questions. And, the worst of the worst, what if I get hung up on? It's not as bad as it seems. First of all, less than 2 % of the people you call will hang up on you. And that may be a high number. In a week that would be a maximum of 5 people out of 250. The key to having a successful phone call is preparation. Remember to focus on your purpose: To introduce yourself and to find out what it will take to do business with them.

IT'S ALL ABOUT YOU
The prospects care about you in relationship to how it's going to help them in their business. . It's your job to help them reach their goal. Find out what their goals are. Always think of yourself as a consultant. You're a new consultant, but you're a consultant. You deserve to get paid. You're going to take the time to get to know their business; what they do, how you can truly help them achieve their goals. "Mr. Shipper, if I put you in a vehicle that's going to help you reach your goal, would you give me an opportunity"? Listen, the first couple of calls, it's always going to be about rates. When you get to rates, just tell them, I've researched the market, - and research the market; really know what the market is, what the high is, what the low is, what the fuel surcharge is - and "Mr. Shipper, I'd rather explain to you one time how I come up with my rates than try to compete with people by dropping my rates by 5 cents a mile or 10 cents a mile, and have to apologize for poor service over and over again. So, with me what you're going to get if the load's not delivered on time, I'm going to let you know. Now I can't drive that truck, and I can't promise you perfect service, but I can promise you perfect communication, and that's what we're all about." That's the sales call you need to make. That's the goal of every traffic manager. They know that things happen. What they want to know is, they want to know about it before it affects their job. They want to know about it before their boss calls them and says, where's my load? Once you get the load, always

communicate, be it by email, by phone call. You make your customers during the hard times. It's easy when everything's going just smooth, but when the trucker calls and says, I'm not going to make delivery, we're going to shut down the assembly line, you be the first person to pick up the phone, call the customer, tell them the truth - that's when you'll make a customer for life.

Self-Confidence

The most critical element for being successful in this endeavor is self-confidence. Self-confidence is gives you a positive yet realistic views of yourself and your situations. Self-confident people trust their own abilities, have a general sense of control in their lives, and believe that, within reason, they will be able to do what they wish, plan, and expect. HAVE AN I CAN DO IT ATTITUDE! If you currently don't have the confidence you need, you can build it. Push yourself to take risks. Approach new experiences as opportunities to learn rather than as a win or lose situation. This opens up new possibilities to succeed. If you don't take a risk, you won't have the opportunity to succeed.

Making the Call

When making a call to a prospect: Call and ask for the Shipping Manager Introduce yourself. Say: Good morning! This is Give Your Name. How are you? I'm a Freight Broker with XX Logistics. Do you have a few minutes to talk? If they say yes, move to the next step. If they say no, ask them if there is a better time to call back. What if I get Voice Mail? Leave the same response. Tell them your name; what you do, your purpose for calling, and leave a phone number and a time you will call back. There are four primary reasons for calling customers beyond the initial contact. They are: What can I do for you today? This call is made on a regular basis to generate business. Confirm past service. This call is made to find out if the client is satisfied with the service they received. Ask about changes. After you have worked with a client, for a while, start having conversations about the client's future. This call should be made at least every 6 months. Educate your client. Keep them informed about what is going on in the industry. Tell them about what is changing in their industry. This will help you secure the role as their expert. These four conversations should be held along with all of the other calls you make just to take care of your day-to-day business.

Establish Credibility
When you make contact with the prospect, you have less than 30 seconds to gain their interest. Again, being prepared is essential. Practice what you are going to say until you can say it without sounding like you are reading it, or making it up as you go along. Here's the process. Give them information about your company. (Why should they do business with you?) Pause and wait for their response. Answer any questions they might have. Ask, May I ask you some questions about your company? Move to step 4.

Develop a Customer Profile
Step 4 is to use the Client Profile to collect information about your client. There are four major areas where information must be gathered. Contact Information, Qualifying Information, Equipment/Service Requirements, and Competitive information. Starting from the first phone call, collect information for the profile. The best way to start is to ask for their permission. If they agree, then start asking questions. If they don't have time, ask for a specific time when it would be more convenient. If they are still reluctant, wait until your next call and try again.

Establish Needs
Step 5 requires that you determine the needs of the prospect. What is important to this prospect? What are their expectations? How do they define service? Every client has different needs. Some care about problems being solved quickly. Some want fast service. Others care about how you treat their client. You must focus on their needs. Use open-ended questions to find out. Open-ended questions require more than a yes or no. They require the person asked to respond by disclosing needed information. For example, instead of saying, How many trucks do you send out each day? you should ask, Could you tell me about your truck volume? With the open question, you will get more than the number of trucks. You may also learn about trends, strategies, the company's plans and other critical information. Use the customer profile as a guide of

areas to explore. Expand your knowledge through open-ended questions.

Customer Retention

The single most important step in this process is to make sure you retain or keep the client. This is best done by following the following strategies: When problems arise, solve them ASAP! Always be available for your client. If you don't respond to their needs, you will lose their business. There are many other brokers that would love to take it from you. Listen more than you talk. Remember, the client determines what service means. I you don't listen to what they are telling you, then you will only be guessing. Be consistent. Make the commitment to your client that they feel safe knowing that your level of service will always remain constant, day-after-day. Make service a pleasure, not a drab. Don't make demands on your clients. Anticipate the customer's needs. Call them before they call you.

Permission Based Sales

You call a lot of people during the day. It's so important to, number one, get to the decision maker. Make sure you get to the traffic manager, or the person who is responsible for freight moving in and out of their facility. Then, when you do get to that person, ask them, Is this a good time for you? Show respect for their time - they will respect it. Take notes. If they do let you in, then ask open ended questions about their business, listen to them. Ask questions like: Do you ship full or partial loads? How many per week? Do you have dedicated lanes? "What we're trying to do, is we're trying to find out if there's anything I can do for you, Mr. Customer, today, or any day, that will help you - so I would like to ask you some questions about your business." You're not going to get the business until you have established the relationship, and until you have earned the trust. Well how do you do that over the phone? You do what you say you're going to do when you say you're going to do it. Bottom line- JUST BE HONEST!

Chapter
3

Your Business Name

One of your first and most challenging steps will be to come up with some options for your business name. Many studies have been conducted regarding business names. Business naming firms can charge thousands of dollars, and can do months of market research in order to come up with names for businesses and products. Keep in mind that by choosing a business name, you are creating a brand, or an identity, for your company. Even if you are not worried that your name becomes a nationwide brand, you will still want your name to be remembered in your own business arena.

Finding a Name

Studies have shown that business names that have initials or numbers are the most easily forgotten. Try to come up with a name that is different, one that says something about your business, or the services you offer. A catchy name, a name with an easily remembered descriptive word, will help you be remembered. Words such as quick, expedited or dependable send a message about your business. Remember, your name will be the first impression. You need to make sure that your name portrays the image that you want to convey. As a freight broker, you will be acting as a consultant for your client, so you want your name and all of your marketing materials to present a professional image. If you begin to see and portray yourself as a professional consultant, others will also. It is also a good idea to have a name that is easy to spell and pronounce. Make sure it is easy to pronounce and understand. Remember that you will be answering the phone with your business name, so think of how it sounds when you pick up the phone.

You might also want to consider the length of your name. Will it fit on your letterhead or business card – does it sound too long to answer the phone with, or could I answer with a shortened version? While you are brainstorming on names, it is a good idea to come up with at least 15 to 20 options, and then narrow them down to two or three. You don't want to get set on one name, only to find out later that it is already taken. You can also get feedback from friends and family to see what appeals to other people. In addition, one of the laws regarding freight brokers says that any advertising that a broker does shall show the broker status of the operation, in order to prevent misrepresentation disputes. It is a great idea to include the word "Logistics" in your business name. This indicates a brokerage or a third party service. Then, if there are ever any disputes, you have represented yourself as a broker in your first contact with each client. Make sure you continue to include that you are a brokerage in all of your other advertising as well. If you are going to specialize exclusively in a certain market, it can be a good idea to include your specialization in your name. However, if you plan to expand into other areas in the future, you might want to make sure that your name is not too limiting.

Some other helpful tips about names are: Straightforward or memorable business names are both good choices. Try not to pick anything too trendy that might become dated. . In general you will want to choose a name that evokes a positive feeling.

Once you have a good list of prospective business names, you can then research trademarks to make sure that your name is still available. Trademarks laws protect companies from having other companies use their name, logo, tagline or motto, or other characteristic markings on similar offerings. You can do a web search with the U.S. Patent and Trademark Office, or you can also go to networksolutions.com and go to the "who is" section.

Business Internet Domain Name
One of the first things you will need to do is to choose your domain name. Try to keep it simple, short and uncomplicated. You want the customer to be able to remember it easily. It's also very important that it is easy to spell. Stick with choosing a .com instead of .net or .org. The .com is used for business and is the easiest for people to remember. A company's internet name can be different from their business name. If you have a catchy name, such as a name that when someone hears it once, they can remember it at a later date and go to your website, you are way ahead of the game. Other tips for choosing your web name: 15 letters or less. You will need to register your chosen name for a very modest fee. The domain registry sites will guide you through the registration. You can register for one year or for multiple years – normally it is a better value to register for multiple years. Once you register your name, no one else can use it as long as you maintain your registration. These registration sites

also offer other useful services, such as domain forwarding, which can direct traffic to a designated page or website.

Business Logo
It is important, because it is always associated with your name on all of your marketing materials. A good logo is a memorable one, and often one that portrays a feeling, typically a warm or positive feeling. You can brainstorm on different sketches and word possibilities for your logo, and it's a great idea to consult with a graphic designer for the final creation of your logo. A graphic designer can also help you with your overall corporate identity.

Setting Up Your Business
There are many different business types to choose from. As your decision will be based on your own personal tax situation, ultimately you will have to make the decision. It is highly recommended that you consult with an accountant and an attorney for advice before making your final decision. These decisions impact how you are taxed, the amount of paperwork your business must do, your liability, and your ability to raise money later. It is more difficult to change the structure of how your business is set up later, than it is to set it up the right way when you are first starting the business.

Types of Businesses
There are 5 basic types of businesses that you can form. Here is a brief description of each one:

1. **Sole Proprietorship**: This is the simplest business structure, which is a business where one person furnishes all of the capital and assumes all of the responsibility and liability. This type of business has a low startup cost, high degree of freedom from regulation, direct control by the owner and all of the profits go to the owner. One benefit is that you have complete control. You make all of the decisions. The downside is unlimited personal liability for any business debts or liabilities. It lacks continuity. The business ceases to exist upon the death of the owner, and it can be difficult to raise capital. If you want to grow or add employees, you

should examine other corporate legal forms. Typically, a sole proprietor will register their business as a DBA ("doing business as" name) with the county business registrar's office, and will pay a nominal fee. This "dba" document is all that the owner needs to open a business bank account in their business name. If you as the owner are the only one conducting business, you can use your social security number in lieu of registering for a federal EIN (tax) number.

2. **Partnership:** A partnership can be a simple arrangement between parties. If partners are investing in your company but won't be managing it with you, you can form a "limited partnership". This is where their financial exposure is limited to the amount of money that they have invested in the company. In a general partnership, each partner is personally liable for all of the debts and responsibilities of the business. A partnership is good for increased cash flow and managerial duties. However, a partnership agreement is highly recommended to make sure that there are no misunderstandings regarding profits, liabilities, responsibilities, and dissolution of the company down the road. A good business attorney can help draw up your partnership agreement. You will want as many details as possible worked out at the beginning.

3. **Corporation:** To set up a corporation you must file Articles of Incorporation with the state office that grants and approves corporate charters. In a corporation, the liability of the owners is limited to the amount that they pay for their shares of stock. A corporation is considered its own legal entity, and its continuity is unaffected by death or shares of stock by any or all owners. The corporation, not the owners, incurs the businesses' debts and assumes its liabilities. The corporation, however, is closely regulated, more expensive to organize and has double taxation on its profits. Tax is levied on both corporate profits and on dividends paid to the shareholders. Most corporations are required to have a Board of Directors, which meets at least once a year.

4. **S Corporation & LLC**: The S Corp is similar to a corporation; however, profits are passed through to the individual shareholders, much in the same way as a partnership. The result being, that there is no federal income tax to the corporation as an entity. This business type is very popular with small business. LLC (Limited Liability Company): Similar to an S Corp, an LLC gives the same liability and tax advantages without all the protocol of a corporation. A LLC can be formed in one easy step, does not have to hold annual meetings or keep minutes, can split profit and loses any way they choose and can be owned by any combination of individuals or business entities.

Consult a professional accountant and attorney for assistance if you need to.

Register Your Business

Once you determine your business type, the next step is to register that business. There are companies, accountants and attorneys that will do this for you, for a fee and they can be found in the yellow pages and on the Internet. If you would like to save the fees and register yourself, it is easy: In most states, to file for a "dba", you register at your County Courthouse. Corporation: To set up a corporation, you must file Articles of Incorporation with the state office that grants and approves corporate charters. You can be set up by going to your state's web site, finding "doing business in/or the corporate link, printing the application and mailing it in with a processing fee. Corporate Charter: This is the document prepared when a corporation is formed. The Charter sets forth the objectives and goals of the corporation, as well as a complete statement of what the corporation can and cannot do while pursuing these goals. This can be procured through an attorney or written by the officers of the corporation. This would usually include the distribution of stock and starting a book for the meeting minutes. A tax ID (EIN) number can be obtained by going to the Internal Revenue Service's web site and following the instructions.

Cash Requirements

How much cash flow do you need if you are going to open a freight brokerage? If you are going to work as an agent? If you are going to open a brokerage, in addition to the $75,000 surety bond that you are required to have in place before you can be licensed, you will need some equipment and transportation software. You need to either have a bank loan, investment cash, or investors, to ensure that you have enough resources for your cash flow requirements. Continual cash flow is one of the most crucial elements of the freight brokerage business. Without ample cash reserves, a brokerage cannot continue to operate and move freight. Cash is the lifeblood of the freight brokerage – because this is the way that it works: The shipper assigns the load to the broker, who then assigns the shipment to the carrier. The shipper pays the broker for the shipping, and the broker pays the carrier who hauled the shipment. In a perfect world, the broker would receive payment from the shipper before the bill to the carrier was due. Usually the carrier will get paid before you receive the payment from the shipper, so there is a break in the in the cash flow coming in and going out – and the broker has to carry the receivables during this gap time. If one truckload shipment averages $1000, and one client shipped just 10 truckloads, the broker would already be carrying $10,000 in receivables. If the broker had 5 shippers that week that shipped 10 loads each, he would have receivables of $50,000 built up pretty quickly. So as you can see, the cash requirements for a broker can build up very quickly. If the broker started out with only $50,000, then he would have used up all of his cash reserves, and would not be able to ship any more loads until more cash came in from his clients. If a broker does not make timely payments to the carrier, then the next time he won't have any carriers to pick up loads for him. Many new brokers find that after they start moving more and more freight that it can become increasingly difficult to stay on top of their receivables. The cash just doesn't seem to be coming in from clients as fast as it needs to go out to the carriers. If any of the shippers drag their feet in making payments, it can put a financial strain on the broker if they don't have a well-established source of funds to tap into. There are bank loans, as well as various other means for finding working capital. Here are some other options: SBA: The Small Business Administration (SBA) is another source for business loans. Higher dollar loans are available to new entrepreneurs who have a well-written business plan and good personal credit. As with a bank loan,

SBA loans generally require that you personally guarantee the loan. Partnerships: There is always opportunity for increased cash flow if someone wants to buy into the business. Venture Capital: There are people who invest in companies. These venture capitalists will often loan capital to a business, for some ownership in the company for a limited time, in hopes of getting huge returns on their investment. Often, they will let the owner run the daily operations of the business as he pleases. After a period of time or when their capital is not needed any longer, they can cash out by selling their part for a profit.

Factoring Companies
One common way to create cash flow in the transportation industry is by the use of factoring companies. These companies in essence buy the brokers' receivables and pay the broker immediately, so that they don't have to wait for the shipper's payment to come in for cash flow. The factoring company charges a percentage of the total invoice amount for providing immediate cash, typically in the range of 2 to 5 % - but, the broker doesn't have to wait thirty or forty five days to receive payment from his/her shipper and can make his/her payments to the carrier. After a load is delivered, the broker will send an invoice to both the shipper and the factoring company. The factoring company will pay the broker immediately and the shipper, under the broker's instruction will pay the factoring company directly according to the terms. This is done on a per load basis, so there is less risk involved, since there are no large loans involved.

Freight Agent
If you are going to open an agency, as a freight agent you will not be required to put up the $75,000 broker bond, or file the $300 + associated fees for your broker's operating authority, since you will be operating under the authority of an established brokerage that will already have these credentials. In addition, you will not be responsible for carrying the receivables from your clients – that will be the duty of your brokerage. Opening a freight agency involves very little start-up costs and equipment. You will have your office set-up costs, a computer with high speed internet, a phone with unlimited long distance service, a fax, a printer, and supplies. There are also some software packages that you may want to purchase, that can make your job much more effective, and can give your agency

the ability to operate much more efficiently. As an agent, your biggest cost will most likely be your time. This is typically a relationship business based on trust, so it takes time at the beginning of your business, to build up your client database. You will need to plan for this start-up time period, by having some cash reserves put back to carry you through while you are building up your customers, or keep a second job. It can take 12-24 weeks on average disciplined calling and working before a broker or agent begins bringing in a fair amount of revenue. This initial time period, while you are breaking the ice with prospects and building up trust, is the hardest part – and you should prepare yourself for it mentally and financially. You could get lucky and close a big account in your first 30 days, but that is the exception rather than the norm.

Income Will Come...Hold On
Have at least 4 to 6 months of cash savings to carry you through. If you make 50 calls every day for three months. Give yourself three months. That's 3000 phone calls, give yourself three months then you'll make it. So I always tell everybody, so you don't put the pressure on yourself have the money saved up. It is going to take at least 3 months of diligent prospecting and you're going to need some cash flow to live on bottom line. So after you've made it through the startup period and you've done your prospecting, you've set your goals, you've done the work, and now you're starting to get customers. You call the customers, you tell them when there's a problem, you communicate, you build up trust, and they have a relationship with you, now some interesting things start to happen. People start calling you and they start giving you loads. They don't even ask you what your rates are going to be. The know for sure that you're going to give them a fair rate because they know that if they've been giving you loads and they've been using other brokers or other carriers, they know that you know the market. The best thing you can do, first thing in the morning, is to deal with all of your problem loads, call your customers, and now you've got a customer for life, they trust you, then it's almost like a rent house, it's like residual business, you have the same carrier picking up the same load everyday going to the same place because they have to supply their customer. The great thing about this business is it's not a one-time sale. It's not multilevel marketing; it's building up trust,

finding a need, fulfilling that need, helping the traffic manager fulfill their goals, helping the carrier fulfill their goals. How do you help the carrier fulfill their goals? Well, most of the capacity is made up of small owner operated companies with 50 trucks or less. They can't afford to have sales representation in every geographical area; they have to use reputable brokers to get their trucks back home. You could be known as one of those reputable brokers.

Setting Up Office

Setting up your office is always fun because you get to go out and buy all the supplies and tools that you will be using on a daily basis. There are a number of items that you will need to be an effective broker.

Desktop PCs have become very inexpensive and a more current model is preferable but the minimum requirements should be: a 1.2GHz CPU, 256 MB of memory, Windows XP (preferably professional but the home version will do), Read/Write CD to back-up your system if needed, and a 15GB hard disk drive. A fax/scanner machine is essential to a brokerage. Carrier and Shipper information including marketing material and contracts are often still faxed, and the machine will be used on a daily basis. If your printer will be used as much as your fax machine, so a good laser printer is preferable over the ink jet type. A laser printer can print a thousand copies or more with its toner cartridge, whereas an ink jet may not get you one hundred. Although the laser printer has a higher cost to it, you will save money in the long run from the ink cartridges that you would not otherwise have to buy. High speed Internet is a must since you will be navigating the Internet almost as much as you are on the phone. A customer doesn't want to have to wait for your web pages to download off of dial up when you are trying to get him a quick quote. Your office should be a room that is comfortable to you, quiet and away from any distractions.

Software for Posting and Rating: You can subscribe to internet based shipment posting and rating services such as internettruckstop.com, which will allow you to view current nationwide rates on all lanes for your shipments. This is a valuable tool, since it would be a full-time job trying to keep up with nationwide lane prices all over the country – and you can lose money if you don't know what the current rates are, in a supply and demand economy. You can also post your available load on the service, and carriers that are interested in your load will contact you. If you are an agent, your broker may purchase this for you, or make it available to you at a reduced rate.

Database Management Software. Many brokers and agents find that database manager/sales software is very useful in keeping up with their prospecting calls and marketing.

Business Image
In any new business, of utmost importance is letting potential customers know that you are open for business, and that you offer more than your competitors. Research shows that a consumer needs to hear of a company, product or service 17 times before they'll remember them. That's 17 opportunities to build your reputation or conversely, lose a sale. In every marketing attempt you must show integrity and professionalism. You must stand out in the crowd of messages. A Freight Broker builds his business through relationships with shippers. Think through the kind of companies you'd like to market to, and build a relationship with, then consider how best to reach them and convince them that you will go above and beyond in serving their needs.
It will be worth your money to work with a professional in developing your business identity, your advertising package and brochure, and talk through your marketing plan and strategies. You will always want a professional image, whether you are representing yourself on the phone or through your marketing materials, and you want that same professional image to be relayed in all of your marketing materials. You want your image to the public to be as consistent as possible. As a consultant, a polished image will give you great credibility. You may be working out of your home office or garage, but professional materials will give you an established look.

Marketing
There are also many computer programs available to help in marketing planning as well as production. In order to develop your

own individual business identity, you need to first identify who you want your target market to be. Your target market is the segment of business that is most likely to need your service. Sure all companies that ship stuff may need a freight broker or agent, but you can't service them all - so you need to find your niche. What kind of brokerage or agency do you want to have?

Target Market
Narrowing your target market as much as possible will also save you marketing dollars and time – instead of shooting for every long shot out there. Narrowing your market will give you a specialization. You want to become an extension of your customer's market, a part of their team. You will want to learn as much as you can about your customer's line of business, so that when you converse you will speak intelligently. They will choose you as their freight broker when they are confident you understand their unique shipping needs.

Advertising
After you have started determining and developing your business identity as a freight broker, you will then need to consider different forms of advertising, public relations, networking, and direct sales in order to get your name in front of the desired market. You will also want to create a fabulous website.

Chapter
4

Marketing and Rates

Marketing is how you present your company to the public. Before you begin your prospecting, or looking for shippers, you need to put together a Shipper Packet, to have ready to send out to potential clients that show an interest in your services. The most effective way to set up the documents in your packet is in a format so that they can be sent instantaneously via email. This way your prospect can receive your information immediately, and you don't have to wait for postal mail. Emailing your Shipper Packets also saves you time printing, addressing envelopes, and postage money. You might consider sending a letter out to these prospects on your second or third contact with them, to change up your marketing avenues. A letter, postcard, or small brochure is also less costly to send in the mail than your entire packet. What should you include in your initial Shipper Packet?

1. **An Introduction Letter**. First of all you want to prepare a letter of introduction for your prospect. Some important things to include in your Introduction Letter are: a) include your logo at the top or the bottom of the letter with your address, phone and fax numbers; b) include your website if you have one and c) include both your business and email address.

2. **Include Some Initial Marketing Information.** Your marketing can be fairly simple at the beginning, such as one or two pages with your mission statement, and the services that you offer, such as truckload, tracking, expedited shipments, and any specialties or specialized equipment. You also want to use your logo on all of your materials to build up your name recognition. Each letter and fax should have your logo on it with all of your contact information, plus your tag line, if you have one. Every email should have your logo and contact information at the bottom, and all of your documents and forms should look as professional as possible.

3. **Include any Rate Information Requested by Your Prospect**.

4. **Include a copy of your Broker's License and a copy of your Surety Bond (or Trust Fund).**

5. **Include a W-9 copy with your taxpayer information.**

6. **Include a Shipper Customer Credit Application**. You must receive this application to receive credit back from your client in order to run his credit report. The results will allow you to

determine his creditworthiness and decide on the dollar amount of credit that you want to extend to him. You need as much information as possible on the client. Make sure that the signature is from an officer of the company. As a broker, you are extending your client a loan on his shipping and once the freight is delivered to the recipient, you have no collateral for your loan to him. Therefore, you must check out his payment history via a credit report and by checking transportation company credit references.

The last thing that we want to discuss regarding your Shipper Packet is a **Broker-Shipper Agreement.** Over the years, carriers have entered into contracts with their brokers, but shippers have not historically signed contracts with brokers. One of the trends effecting our industry right now is brokers are trying to get contracts with shippers, the Transportation Intermediary Association which is the TIA, they have shipper contracts, you can go to a lawyer and get a shipper contract the way it's been done is the bill of lading is the legal document. The shipper puts on the bill of lading what the product is, the carrier signs the bill and agrees that the product is on there and that it's exactly the same amount as the shipper says it is and then when the freight is delivered the consignee actually looks at the freight bill of lading and says yes I did receive exactly what's on the freight bill and they sign it; and so that's the legal document. The brokers are trying to go to shipper contracts and the shippers, some will and some won't. Now the ones that will, would be your fortune 500 companies when you do a bid package for someone and you're moving hundreds and thousands of loads and you've bid on this one lane for a year, they'll sign a contract with you. And that would mean that you're going to get this amount of business. But the smaller companies, most likely won't sign a contract that says I'm going to do business with you Mr. Broker because they really don't need to, and that's the reality of it.

Carriers

Once you make contact with a motor carrier that you are interested in contracting with, to move a shipment (or shipments) for you, you will send them your carrier packet, via email or fax, so that you can set them up in your database. You will need to prepare your carrier packet ahead of time and have it ready before you begin prospecting.

You will start a new carrier file for each carrier that you contract with, and you will start the file with the information that you receive back from the carrier. You need this information to make sure that you have a legal master contract on file with the carrier before you begin doing business with them. You will also need proof in their file that they are a legal, authorized motor carrier by obtaining a copy of their motor carrier operating authority. You also need proof that they have ample, valid cargo insurance. Obtain a copy of their insurance coverage certificate showing their insurance coverage, which you must then verify. You will also want to check their safety rating.

Carrier Packet

List of suggested information to include in your carrier packet. Start each new carrier file with this information. Include: Request for copy of Carrier's Operating Authority. Request for copy of their Insurance Certificate requiring minimum cargo liability limits of $100,000 and minimum liability coverage of $1,000,000, listing your brokerage company as a certificate holder. Broker/Carrier Agreement (this is your Master Contract) with request to be signed and returned promptly. Blank W-9 form. Blank Carrier Profile for them to fill out. Include a copy of your own Broker Authority & Bond. Include your References. Send trade references if you have been in this industry, if available; if you are new, send them banking references, or references from any other company you have owned, or personal credit information. Copy of your "Quick Pay" carrier option (optional; use only after you have ample cash flow).

Carrier's Authority

Let's talk about the items in your carrier packet. The first item, a request for a copy of the Carrier's Operating Authority, will provide you with their Motor Carrier (MC) number from the Department of Transportation, so that you can determine that they are a legally authorized motor carrier, and you can check on their safety records. You can check on www.safersys.org.

Insurance

The second item, a request for a copy of the carrier's

insurance certificate, with minimum coverage requirements requested, should list your brokerage as a certificate holder, and should show that the carrier has ample cargo insurance (a minimum of $100,000) and liability ($1,000,000), which means that your clients' shipments with this carrier are insured. You will need the insurance certificate of the carrier on file, but since insurance coverage on your clients' shipments is critical, in addition to receiving the carrier's insurance certificate, as part of your due diligence, you should also make a quick check call to the insurance provider listed on the certificate, before each shipment, to make sure that the policy is valid and current and that no lapse has occurred.

Broker-Carrier Agreement

The next item in the packet is your Broker-Carrier Agreement, which is the Master Contract between you and the carrier. It is a critical document that you have on file for each carrier, because it spells out all of the terms and agreements made between you and the carrier for the shipments that you tender to that carrier. Any special provisions or procedures that you want should be included in this agreement. You will only need to get this Master Contract signed once from your carrier, and it will be good for as long as you do business together. You do not need a separate Broker-Carrier Contract for each shipment that you move with this carrier, as it is an ongoing contract. After you have this master contract on file, you will then have a one page "Confirmation of Rate Agreement" sheet for each individual shipment that you arrange with the carrier. This Rate Agreement will reference the individual shipment number, show the rate agreed upon between the broker and the carrier, and will be an addendum to the Master Contract.

The Load

It is important to know that before you start discussing any specifics about your shipper, your client's commodity, or the pickup location, you must first have this signed Master Contract from the carrier in your possession. The reason is because, if you do not have a signed contract to protect you, you are disclosing important information to the carrier and you have no contract in place yet to protect you from the carrier calling on your customer directly and cutting you out altogether. It may not be ethical for the carrier to go and call on your client at this point, but you would have no legal leg to stand on in a courtroom, because you had no signed contract with him. Don't even give hints. For example, if you tell a prospective carrier that you will be moving a truckload of bricks out of Sanford, NC to Wilmington, NC, the carrier may know that there is only one large brick company in Sanford, NC –or, he can look it up in a manufacturer's guide. He may just decide to go ahead and try to call on them, and try to cut you out. You thought he was interested in the load, but then you never heard back from him. You may later on see his truck name on trailers in their warehouse yard!   Your signed contract with the carrier is your only protection that you have against this because it will have a "no back-solicitation" clause in it, which states that the carrier is prohibited in the contract from calling on your customer directly.

When the carrier makes an inquiry about the shipment, instead of saying that it is from Sanford use generalities before you have a contract – you can say that it is about 30 minutes outside of Raleigh, NC, and its delivery is about 20 minutes from Wilmington, NC and give them the weight and correct number of miles, which you will look up. As long as they know the general vicinity of the pick-up and destination, and you calculate the correct number of miles, and give them the weight of the shipment; which your customer will tell you; the carrier will know if they are interested in the load. The carrier should understand that the details are not his to know at this point. You don't know each other yet, which they should respect. If the carrier asks what the commodity is, you can say that it is a manufactured product, and that you will get the details on it to him when you have a contract in place. At that point you can email or fax your carrier packet to him, which has your Master Contract in it for him to sign.

Rate Confirmation Sheet

The Rate Confirmation sheet, which is to be generated for each shipment; each Rate Confirmation sheet is an addendum to the Master Contract, for that particular shipment – so it becomes part of the contract. The Rate Confirmation sheet shows the specific rates and terms agreed upon between the broker and the carrier for each shipment. It should also show any specialized equipment requested or special instructions that have been mutually agreed upon. It should be signed by both parties.

The Broker-Carrier Contract

The carrier agrees to maintain satisfactory safety ratings and to remain in compliance with all laws and regulations, and agrees to cease transactions with the broker (and broker's customers) and notify the broker immediately of any changes. Even with this in the Contract, you will want to check your carrier's compliance and safety ratings, to make sure that you are tendering your client's shipments to a safe and reputable carrier. The carrier agrees that it will not re-broker or re-assign any of the shipments, but will transport them under the carrier's own authority. This is an important point, because by law a broker is required to tender the shipment to an "authorized motor carrier". If the carrier that the load was tendered to turned around and tendered it to someone else, then the original broker would not know if it was necessarily tendered to an authorized and insured motor carrier – which could open him up for negligence. The carrier shall provide adequate insurance coverage, including a minimum of $100,000 in cargo insurance and $1,000,000 in liability insurance including property damage and personal injury. This insurance is extremely important, because the carrier must have primary insurance – because the broker cannot carry primary insurance on the cargo, since he never handles the load at any time, just as a real estate agent couldn't be responsible if a roof fell in, on a house that he was the broker for. Legally, the broker is not responsible for insurance claims, unless he is negligent in some way. The carrier agrees not to attempt to collect any freight charges directly from broker's customers. There are also restrictions on the carrier regarding any direct solicitation of broker's customers or consignees. The "Back-solicitation" clause is one of the most important clauses in the contract, as it protects you from the carrier calling directly on your clients. This clause should be discussed with the transportation attorney who drafts your contracts. This sample contract calls for a 15% commission to the broker from the carrier for one year, if this clause is breached, as well as the right for the broker to enforce the covenant by restraining order and to collect actual damages from the carrier. This clause should be as strict as your attorney will allow, as it is your main protection of your revenue. The carrier needs to communicate with the broker by requiring a "check call" at least once a day, to notify you of the location of the shipment. The contract should also be confidential. As a broker, your Master Contract is probably the most important document that you will have in place. In addition to having it drafted by a specific transportation attorney, due to periodic changes in specific laws and court rulings, it is a good idea to have it reviewed and edited by your attorney on a regular basis. In addition, you will want to provide a blank W-9 for the carrier to fill out and return his taxpayer information, a blank Carrier Profile for him to fill out showing all of his contact information (including emergency #s), and equipment and service areas that he specializes in, a copy of your broker's license and surety bond (or trust fund) for his files, a list of your credit references, your general office information, and an "Easy Quick Pay Option" (optional) for the carrier. We will discuss the option of offering a quick pay option for your carriers in the Accounting section.

Competitive Rates

As a new broker or agent, how do you determine your prices? How do you know what fair market rates are? As shippers are being quoted, they have a tendency to automatically say that the rate is too high, and then we fall into the trap of reducing our price to the point of not being able to find a carrier. After finishing this section, you should have enough knowledge and tools to use to become confident in the rates that you quote.

The most important thing when generating a rate quote is getting accurate information about the load from the shipper the first time. It's common for a new agent/broker to neglect getting all the needed information and have to make several follow up calls to the shipper. This does not create confidence in the shipper. The information that you will need to create accurate truckload rate quotes is:
1. Pick-up and Destination information including Dates and Times.
2. Any Additional Stops to be made before final Destination Delivery.
3. Type of Truck needed (reefer, dry van, or flatbed).

4. Commodity (Product Type) and Value of Shipment.
5. Weight.
6. How much the Shipper normally pays.
7. Are there any Special Requirements needed?

Once the load information is established, work can begin on the quote.

As a new broker or agent, how do you determine your prices? How do you know what fair market rates are? Truckloadrate.com is a great website for telling you what the market rates are. Since there is nothing solid to compare a rate to, it sometimes feels as if we are shooting blind. A good rule of thumb is to always quote off of the median rate rather than the high or low rate, because you want to be fair and give your shipper a good price. It is always easier to re-quote later if you find out that your rate is too high, rather than to have to go back to your shipper and ask for more money because you can't find a carrier that will run your load for that amount.

Rates may also vary due to circumstances and events. Some examples of rate variables are: 1. Supply and Demand: One important rate variable is always supply and demand in a given area, which is true of any commodity in our economy. If the ratio of available trucks to available shipments in the area is high, then the price will be lower.

Head haul and Back Lanes
A head haul is when a carrier has a load and is leaving the place of origin (his home base), or is leaving a high industry state (high freight volume area). Areas with higher demand for trucks command a premium rate. A backhaul is when the carrier wants to return home, or is in an area where industry is low, and he will take a lower rate. So, a backhaul is the return trip of a vehicle from the destination back to the origin, or to another desired location. A discounted rate applies where there are a lot of inbound trucks, but not enough freight to load them. Intermediate hauls are where supply and demand are about equal - the rates are average.

Dead haul or Deadhead

This is the distance a carrier may have to drive to pick up a load without any revenue. In other words, he may have to drive 50 miles from where he currently is to pick up his next load. Seasonality: Some states, such as Florida, have little or no manufacturing and therefore command a higher rate. Since the carrier knows that he may have to wait for a load, he may have to dead haul a long way or he may not get a load out. However, during Florida's growing season, when produce is at its peak, rates to Florida decrease because produce loads are available on the carrier's backhaul.

Van Types

Type of Van: As mentioned earlier, the type of van being used may increase the rate. Two examples would be reefers and tankers. Reefers use more energy to run the truck and tankers are more scarce. They also may be hauling hazardous material as well. More specialized equipment normally equates to higher freight rates. Type of Commodity or Product: Normally, cheaper products (such as raw fiber, or recyclables) mean less expensive freight rates, due to lower liability, and high dollar products (pharmaceuticals or computers, for example) cost more to ship.

Tolls & Short hauls

Tolls and Taxes: Truck tolls are often forty or fifty dollars and some states require a fee or tax to be paid upon entering that state. These fees come out of the driver's pocket and of course, rates may be higher if there are a lot of tolls involved. Short haul: Generally, carriers do not like short hauls under five or six hundred miles, since they can make more money on a long haul. Rates will be at a premium for a carrier to take that short run unless it is a backhaul and he wants to go home. The carrier may also have a minimum rate established for any load as well.

Services

If you can offer services that are unique, then you are more likely able to influence the price that you receive. This is actually the opposite of just offering just a plain commodity. Be creative and add as many "value-added" services that you can think of, to help your client, or specialize by "niche" marketing. These services will give you better opportunities than low cost driven pricing. As a broker or an agent, you are not going to be the cheapest on the block, so you need to sell service over price. If you try to be the cheapest, someone will undercut you by a few pennies.

Profit Margins

It is a good idea to decide ahead of time what your minimum profit margins will be, and your goal. One suggestion would be to set a minimum profit margin for yourself of 15%-20%. You want to remain fair to all parties involved.

Fuel Surcharge

A broker or agent will very often ask the carrier to quote the shipment with the fuel surcharge already built into the rate, so that there are no unknown variables in what the total invoice will be. The fuel surcharge is passed directly on to the customer's price with no mark-up. Truckloadrate.com gives you the option of adding the fuel surcharge in or not. This type of quote is called "all in" when you quote the shipment plus the fuel surcharge.

Other Fees

Finally, there are the other extra fees that may be added to the rate, but these are often not realized until after the load is delivered. These would include: 1. Lumper Fees: A fee that is charged by the carrier if he has to pay out of pocket to have the truck unloaded. 2. Detention Charge: If a carrier has to wait for an extended period of time after his appointment for pick-up or delivery, he may charge a fee. Generally, any wait over two hours will get a detention charge. 3. Equipment ordered but not used: If a truck is ordered and not canceled at least four hours prior to pick-up, a fee is generally imposed. 4. Extra Stops: Additional stops normally require an extra stop fee. 5. Tarp charge: There may be an additional charge for tarps (generally used with flatbeds).

Flat and Weight Rates

There are several types of rate quotes used for various situations, which include: 1. Flat Rate: This rate includes any and all other rates. The flat rate is the simplest, and will be the most accurate, since there are no unknown variables. 2. Weight: This type of rate, usually used in produce distribution, is based on the weight of the actual items being hauled. In the case of produce, the more weight a carrier can haul, the more he gets paid. An example of this type of formula would be: A shipper will pay $5.00 per 100 lbs. Assuming the carrier can load 42,000 lbs., $5.00 x 420 = $2,100. The shipper will pay the carrier $2,100.00 to haul 42,000 lbs. of produce.

Chapter
5

Load Data
Once you have found a prospect that requests a rate quote on a shipment, you need to gather the load information. You need to get this information from the shipper up front, so you don't have to keep calling back for missing bits of information. Ask the shipper for the load details. What information do you need to obtain from your client? You will want to ask if the shipper has an order or purchase order number (if the customer uses P.O. #s). Find out information on the pick-up point of the shipment - full address, phone and fax, contact(s), email, directions, hours of operation, after hours contact info. The pick-up date and what would be an available window of time to pick up the shipment. What the product type is (also called the commodity). The weight of the product. The value of the shipment. What the equipment requirements are. Are there any additional stops besides the final delivery? If there are extra stops, you will need to get all of the same information for each stop such as address, phone & fax, and directions. Include stop charges on the quote, all of the information on the final delivery point (same information as the pick-up). For Delivery information needed or any special instructions such as if a delivery appointment is required or extra charges. Information for the billing: where to bill, address, contact(s) information, phone #, email) This information will be added into your transportation operations software screen, along with the carrier information on whichever carrier that you assign the load to.

Special Instructions
While you are compiling your load data on a shipment from a customer, you want to make sure you ask for and understand any special instructions. Ask a lot of questions about your client's operations, and their shipments, so that you are aware of any special situations or specialized equipment needed. Many times your only special instructions might be that a delivery appointment is required and must be adhered to, at one or all of your pickup and delivery points. Or it could be that your shipper requires a 53' van instead of a 48'. They are more difficult to locate. If you don't listen and send out a 48' trailer, your carrier might be turned away. Occasionally, you have a shipper with special situations that require special instructions for your carrier. You may possibly need to add to your

contract with your carrier, if there are strict guidelines to be followed.

Restrictions and Late Fees
If the client has restrictions or late fees, this should be explained to the carrier and should be put in writing as specifications on the rate confirmation with the carrier. Every special situation or instruction should be in writing with the carrier, so that everything is clear. If it is critical, you may have to include a penalty in your contract with the carrier for late delivery. Just make sure that you make this clear with the carrier ahead of time, and that it is in the contract. Don't ever solicit restrictions from your shippers though. You'll be making it harder on yourself, and harder on the carrier! Just find out if they have any restrictions, so that you or your carrier won't be blind-sided.

Special Situations
What are some other examples of special situations? Special wraps needed. Product cannot be put on truck with any other product. Trailer must be clean, dry and odor-free or reefer units may need to be held at a certain temperature. Many shippers won't have any unusual or out-of-the-ordinary special situations. However, there are plenty of special situations that can exist, depending on the client. Just be ready! As you get to know your client, ask as many questions as possible. Listen carefully to come up with creative solutions to their shipping dilemmas. Remember that you are a consultant for the shipper – become the professional. The more problems that you help your shipper solve, and the easier that you make his job, the more valuable that you become. Always focus on how you can help improve your client's shipping department. Become a part of their team – the one with solutions.

Rate Verification
Once you have agreed on the price with your client, along with any other parameters required on the shipment, you should get a signed rate quote verification from them, sent to you via fax or email. Make sure that it is signed by both parties – the client and you. The customer's signature is proof of their acceptance of the terms of the quote. Remember that time is of the essence with shipping. The

quicker that you can get this one handled, the quicker that you can go on to work on the next shipment. You need to create a sense of urgency so that you will receive all of the paperwork back to you as soon as possible, and you can keep the ball rolling. Time is money in this business.

Rate Confirmation

Each individual shipment will have its own individual rate confirmation, which will have a load reference number that coordinates to the load reference number assigned to the load from your transportation software. This reference number should be on any paperwork pertaining to this load from start to finish, so that it will be easy to look up at any time. If you have a sequence of loads from the shipper, shipping on the same day to the same destination, with the same product on each truck, they can be assigned a series of reference numbers, which could be referenced in one rate verification with your client. Just make sure that all of the information is the same if you use only one rate confirmation for a series of loads.

Extra Fee Sheet

Make sure that you have verified the shipment's weight and estimated load value with the client, and include this information in with your rate confirmation. The load value is extremely important, because you need to verify that your carrier's insurance covers the load value amount. If the load value exceeds the carrier's cargo insurance limits, that is typically $100,000 in coverage. An additional insurance rider needs to be purchased to cover the value, unless the shipper is self-insured and willing to sign a statement stating such. They should sign a release of liability for any amount above $100,000, if they opt not to purchase additional coverage. In the rare event the shipment is stolen along with its documents, the rate confirmation agreement is your paperwork backup that shows what was actually on the truck, and it verifies the dollar amount that was lost.

Load Value

Make sure that you have verified the shipment's weight and estimated load value with the client, and include this information in with your rate confirmation. The load value is extremely important, because you need to verify that your carrier's insurance covers the load value amount. If the load value exceeds the carrier's cargo insurance limits, that is typically $100,000 in coverage. An additional insurance rider needs to be purchased to cover the value, unless the shipper is self-insured and willing to sign a statement stating such. They should sign a release of liability for any amount above $100,000, if they opt not to purchase additional coverage. In the rare event the shipment is stolen along with its documents, the rate confirmation agreement is your paperwork backup that shows what was actually on the truck, and it verifies the dollar amount that was lost. If you forgot to ask, and the truck turned up missing, who knows what dollar value was on that truck? It could be any amount – you need a written verification ahead of time. This rate verification serves as a contract between you and the shipper on this load. Pay attention that all details are documented.

Load Posting

Now that you have negotiated an agreeable rate with the shipper and obtained all of your load data, it is time to find a carrier. Posting the load on the internet with a load matching service is the fastest way to find a carrier. There are many load posting boards and services available, where you can type in your load, and your available shipment will show up on the internet, and on truck stop posting screens, along with your contact phone number, for trucking companies to view. Most of the services require a monthly subscription membership fee. However, there are also free load boards. They vary in price from free to up to $200 per month, depending on additional services offered. This is a minimal business price to pay for finding trucks for your loads. Here are a few of the most frequently used internet load boards.

When and What to Post

When you first open your brokerage or freight agency, you will probably post most all of your shipments, unless you have already established relationships with carriers. The earlier you post the load, the better. If you post it early, you have more time to find carriers and to negotiate the rate. You may even find a back-up carrier in case a problem occurs.

Client Communication
As you get to know your clients, try to communicate to them that it will help everyone if they can give you as much lead time as possible to work on a shipment. Explain to them that this will give you more time to match the load up with the right carrier, and will allow you to provide better service. I

Working with Shippers
Sometimes, a shipment might not be critical. If your client says the shipment needs to go out on Thursday, don't assume that the timing is set in stone. If you absolutely can't find a carrier, maybe you know someone who could pick it up on Friday. Call your client. Explain that trucks are in short supply for Thursday. Would it be possible to pick the shipment up on Friday? Sometimes they'll say no and give the shipment to another broker or carrier, but sometimes it will work. You will find out that most customers in today's market won't put all of their eggs in one basket, especially customers with large amounts of freight or time-sensitive freight. They know that demand for trucks often exceeds supply, so they have multiple back-up brokers and carriers. There are also some clients who will blast emails out to everyone on their broker-carrier list when they need a shipment filled. The early bird catches the worm! They'll often give the shipment to whoever can cover it first at a fair price.

Competition
Sometimes you may be working on a load and see that it looks like your same load has been posted by someone else on the internet. If so, it may be a race to the finish. DON'T call your client and tell them that you already have a truck for the load if you don't have it covered yet. Tell them the truth. It is better to give up a load then to be less than truthful with your client. Remember, it is a trust-based business, and you can lose all of your trust and credibility by not being honest with them.

Load Specifics-Don't Post
Don't post the commodity and post the closest large pick-up city and destination city. You can tell the carrier the mileage involved without giving him the specifics on the load until you have a contract

in place. If you give out the specifics without a contract in place, your load could disappear out from under you, because you are disclosing proprietary information. Not everyone is always so honest. You can see how this is a relationship business.

Early Posts
Remember, the early bird catches the worm. If you're posting is visible early in the morning, there are more trucks in the morning that are empty and ready to get on the road. As the morning wears on, most empty trucks will find a load and be on their way, so you are less likely to find a truck. It is also recommended that you leave the price open. You will get more calls. You can negotiate from there. Additionally, if you have multiple loads available in certain regions, you can post by region, so that you'll really be posting multiple loads with one listing.

Reviewing Carrier Documents
Once you have found a carrier, you send out your Carrier Packet to your Carrier. This contains the documents including the master contract. When you receive the requested information from your Carrier Packet, review the material. A thorough review would include the following steps: Check that the Master Carrier-Broker contract that you receive back is signed by both parties. Make sure that their W-9 information is provided. Make sure you have the Carrier's insurance certificate listing your company as a certificate holder. Review the insurance information. Look at the Carrier's profile information since you want to build up a relationship with their company, and check the motor Carrier's Authority and Safety record.

Carrier Authority and Safety
To check the validity of the Carrier's authority, you can go to the Federal Motor Carrier Safety Administration's website, enter the Carrier's name and information, and the status of their Motor Carrier operating authority will pull up. Some of the load boards will also allow you to pull up the Carrier's authority on their site, as a service. You can visit the website www.safersys.org and it will show the Carrier's safety records such as accidents and other violations of the

law. If there are a lot of accidents, or the Carrier is out of compliance, you should contact the Carrier to determine if there is a reason, and ask politely what actions that they are taking to fix any noncompliance issues. If the Carrier doesn't check out, and they are not cooperative when you call them, then you should move on to your next Carrier option.

Due Diligence

However, you can actually be held liable by acting negligently in your operations. Recent court cases have held brokers responsible for their carrier choices, and courts have upheld that it is not too much to expect, for a broker to make sure that a carrier is safe and in compliance. It is extremely important not to cut corners.

Insurance

One of the items to request from the Carrier is a copy of their insurance certificate, showing their insurance limits. Since the Carrier is the one that will be handling the freight, they must carry the primary cargo insurance, and freight claims from your customers will be filed on their insurance. It is critical for you to again do your due diligence in checking that your client's freight is sufficiently insured. Typically, a copy of this certificate will be faxed to you, with your company named under certificate holder, when you are first setting the Carrier up in your system to move a load with him. A follow-up hard copy should come in the mail after this, for your permanent Carrier file.

As soon as you receive the insurance certificate, there are four main points that you need to check for. First, you should check the limits of the Carrier's motor cargo insurance. Make note of any deductible or exclusions shown. This is located at the bottom of the certificate, in the other insurance section. In most cases, you should make sure that the Carrier has a minimum of $100,000 in cargo insurance. This will be ample coverage to cover most average truckloads of freight, unless you are arranging for the shipment of high value products. This is also a prerequisite from the Carrier, in your master Broker-Carrier contract. It is critical that you have verified in writing the shipment's load value with your client. If you have a high value load, and its value exceeds $100,000, then an additional cargo insurance rider will need to be purchased for the shipment. If there is an extremely high deductible, such as $10,000 or $15,000, be aware that any insurance claim under that amount would have to be paid directly by the Carrier. If there are damages, it will be more difficult to get paid, since it would be coming out of the Carrier's pocket, and not covered by insurance. If that is the case, you may want to look for a different Carrier for your load. In addition, you should pay attention to any exclusion shown here by the insurance provider, and make sure that any exclusion would not apply to your client's shipments. For example, it could say that it excludes refrigerated product - and you may be shipping refrigerated product.

Certificate Details
Second, you should make sure that the coverage dates are current and not about to expire. This is imperative to verify that your client's cargo will be currently insured. When you set the Carrier up, you will enter the insurance coverage dates into your transportation software. Most operations software systems will not let you in if you try to use a Carrier whose insurance has expired. You should receive renewal certificates in the mail to replace expired certificates. However, if you have not received one, and you have received an alert in your system, you will need to contact the Carrier to provide you with a current certificate on file. Third, you should make sure that they carry a minimum of $1,000,000 per occurrence in liability insurance. This is a prerequisite in your master Broker-Carrier contract, that the Carrier maintain these minimum limits. Fourth, your brokerage company should be listed under certificate holder on the bottom left part of the certificate. This shows that the loads tendered to the Carrier by broker are covered under this policy. From time to time, you will have a client request that they would like a copy of the insurance certificate showing them as a certificate holder or additional insured. If your client requests this, you will need to request that the Carrier's insurance provider provide you with this for your client. It should be a second certificate showing your client's company on it. Sometimes there is a minimal fee to obtain another certificate.

Insurance Claims and Verification
If there are damages on your shipment and there is a claim, it will first be filed with this insurance provider. It is imperative that you

make sure that this insurance is valid and sufficient, as part of your due diligence. You should only need to request this certificate once from each Carrier – not each time you move a load with them. You keep the certificate in the Carrier's permanent file, and you will be sent their renewal update certificates as time goes on. However, as a checks and balance procedure, you should go ahead and make a quick call to the insurance provider each time that you do a load with the Carrier, to verify that the insurance is still current. Note that in the top fine print of the insurance certificate, there is a disclaimer that says: This certificate is issued as a matter of information only and confers no rights upon the certificate holder. This certificate does not amend, extend or alter the coverage afforded by the policies below. This is only an overview of the policies of the Carrier. It is impossible to know if there are any other exclusions or non-coverage items that might be in the fine print of the policies. Any given policy could have different exclusions in the fine print which you don't see.

Managing Liability
The carrier's policy payment could be late by one day – which could be the day of your shipment! That is why you need to make a quick check call before the truck is dispatched for the load pick up. Include a clause in your master Broker-Carrier contract that says that the carrier must maintain these minimum levels, and must notify you immediately of any policy changes or cancellations. And in the event of cancellation or lapse of policy, the carrier agrees to be responsible for covering any insurance claims not covered by insurance or any exclusion in the policies.

Rate Agreement
You will have a contract addition for each individual shipment between you and your carrier, which spells out the terms and agreements made between you and the carrier on that particular shipment. This is called a carrier rate agreement. The master contract should refer to these individual load rate confirmations as contract addendums; the confirmation of the verbal rate agreement

document should refer back to the master contract. It should also reference your broker load reference number, assigned by your internal operations transportation software, when you begin entering load data on that shipment into your system. If there are any questions, it will be easy to reference the load quickly in your system. Any document generated or correspondence regarding that shipment should include this broker load reference number, so that it is easy to track it back to the correct shipment at any time. Since this is part of your contract, as a broker you should have a transportation attorney draft it for you, along with all of your other business documents that you will be using in the operation of your business. If you decide to work as a freight agent instead of a broker, and work under the umbrella of an existing brokerage, then your broker will be responsible for all of these contracts and documents.

Rate Confirmation
Information that might be included on your rate confirmation sheet with the carrier includes the full name of both the trucking and brokerage companies, your broker load reference number, the origin and destination cities of the shipment and any stops to be made, the total rate agreed upon between you and the carrier, and, as a separate line item, any additional charges that have been mutually agreed upon between you and the carrier if the charge is not included in the base rate listed on your confirmation. The agreed upon payment terms should also be in your master broker-carrier contract/agreement. There will typically be a section in your document for you to add any special notes or agreements. You should be careful to include anything that is discussed if it is not in your master contract agreement. You should state your payment terms and instructions in the note section of the rate agreement. It is also a good idea to add your broker's load reference number on the carrier's invoice to you. This makes it easy to pull the correct load paperwork in your office when the invoice arrives. These are the terms and billing requirements for your carrier.

Notes
Some examples of things that you might want to include in your notes section of your carrier rate agreement: If agreed upon services are not fulfilled, rates are negotiable. If double-brokered, agreement

is canceled! Drivers call your phone #, not the client or consignee for pickup and delivery information. HAVE ALL REQUIREMENTS IN BOLD PRINT SO THEY CAN BE EASILY SEEN.

Remain as Point of Contact
You want to make sure that you have not left anything out that is needed to communicate to the carrier. Make sure that everything is clear and in writing. Don't ever let a situation arise where the carrier has to call the shipper for information. You keep control of your business.

Carrier Pickup and Delivery Schedule
After you receive your signed rate agreement from the carrier, you are ready to send out the carrier pick-up and delivery schedule, and dispatch the truck to its pick up point. This document should include all of the details that the carrier will need for this shipment. Some things to include are: Your complete company and contact information with your broker operating authority #, The carrier's name and information including their MC#, Date and time stamp, A request to refer to your load reference # when billing or inquiring about this load, Any special instructions that you have or that the shipper has. Equipment required, Value of load, Complete information on pick-up including addresses, phone #s, contact(s), pick-up date, commodity, # of pieces, whether appointment is required, load value, and weight. Complete information on any stops required (same information as above) Complete information on delivery. Your billing information and contact(s).

Dispatching the Load
Contact the shipper and confirm the pick-up details, and call the recipient to verify the delivery and to make sure that everything goes smoothly. Use this call as a sales call, always ask if the recipient has any other shipments or anything else you can help with. After you have sent over the carrier pickup and delivery schedule via fax or email, establish contact with the driver, and make sure that he knows the details of the delivery (including directions). **Do not have the driver call the plant for details, including directions. You can**

call if you need to, for directions, and pass them on. Remember that as much as possible you should be the contact with the client. Confirm with the driver that he will call you as soon as he picks up the load, and let him know that you require a daily check call until the load is delivered at the final destination. Each day the delivery is in route, you want to give a tracking report to your client with the status of the shipment. When you first start to establish your relationship with the shipper, we recommend that you make a daily phone call. Check in with your clients and report the status of their loads. Make your call to the recipient within an hour after delivery, or after the driver checks in with you. Report back to your shipper that the shipment has been delivered on time, and in great shape, and again, always ask for more business. If there were any problems, you will want to call your shipper immediately and make him aware of the situation. It is better for your client to hear about any problems from you, instead of hearing it from their customer or boss.

Carrier Relationship

Start a new file for each carrier, with the carrier packet information that is returned to you, when you are setting up the carrier to move your first shipment with them. Since dependable and honest carriers are critical to a successful brokerage operation, you want to constantly work at building up relationships with good carriers. Begin to compile a database of carriers that you want to use on a repeated basis.

Claims

If there is a problem with your client's shipment, there are various types of insurance claims that may be filed. Every insurance claim is a little different, but here are the main categories of freight claims: The first type of claim, visible damages, should be noted on the proof of delivery and is acknowledged by the consignee/receiver and the driver. Visible Damage is damage that is detected by the consignee at the time of delivery. The consignee should write a description of the damages beside his signature when he signs for the freight. If the consignee or carrier notifies you, tell them to please take pictures. For this type of claim, and for most types of cargo insurance claims, the time limit for the customer to file the claim is legally 9 months.

Concealed Damage is when the consignee fails to inspect or overlooks the damage on delivery or damage is not evident by observing the exterior of the container. The damage is detected when the shipment is opened. Call the carrier upon discovery and make a written notation that you called to report the damage.

Delays

A delay is a delivery beyond the normal transit time for a particular type of shipment. Note the precise time and date of delivery. File a claim within the time limit. It is rare but possible for a client to file a delay claim. This is a much more difficult claim to get paid. Typically it will boil down to what it says in the contract between the broker and the carrier regarding late deliveries and fees. If it is in your contract and rate confirmation, before the fact, and the carrier has agreed to it as part of the contract, then the carrier is responsible. However, most contracts say that acts of God are excluded, such as a weather situation. Also, there may well be a clause in the carrier's insurance policy where the insurance provider is not responsible for delays, such as breakdowns. In this case, the carrier who agreed to this contractual term would be the one responsible, and not his insurance provider. It is impossible for you as a broker to know about any exclusion that could be in the fine print of the carrier's insurance policy. Make sure that you have an attorney draft your broker-carrier contract and rate confirmations, so you are protected in these matters.

If you have a customer that says that if you don't deliver on time, it will shut down the plant and cost us $25,000 per hour, you might want to think twice before taking the load. Delays are not uncommon. Most companies that offer guaranteed expedited on-time deliveries, if there is a delay, they will reimburse the freight cost at the most, and you would need a contractual agreement even for that. You can explain to the client that you will expedite the shipping, for an expedited price, and that the delivery will be guaranteed for the amount of the shipping cost -that is if your carrier has agreed to this in the contract. You may be able to get the carrier to agree to an hourly delay fee in your contract, but of course it would be nowhere near $25,000 an hour! Most likely, no one will take on that kind of liability for the client. Just make sure and communicate with everyone ahead of time, and make sure that everyone understands the terms, so that there won't be any misunderstandings. And make sure to include any agreements in signed contracts.

Shortage and Load Tampering

If a delivery is short, the consignee should make note of the amount of the shortage on all copies of the delivery receipt, beside his signature in the presence of the driver. This would be a shortage claim. If there is evidence of pilferage, or the appearance that someone has tampered with the shipment, the consignee must take an inventory jointly with the driver and note the contents that were actually delivered on the delivery receipt or inspection report. The weight of the container must also be noted.

Filing Claims

Any insurance claim that is filed, is filed to the carrier's insurance provider on the certificate of insurance that you received and checked before the carrier moved the load. You may want to contact the carrier first, to make sure that he does not want to pay the claim and not file it on his insurance. If it is a large claim, it would be a good idea not to take any chances of the carrier failing to file the claim with his insurance company. Don't instigate claims. Just facilitate the ones you know will be a claim situation. Always be the first to notify your shipper if possible. You have requested your carrier to notify you immediately of any damages, but it is possible to have something slip through the cracks. Many photographs have solved a claim instantly.

Broker Liability

As a broker or an agent, you cannot be liable for freight damages, since you do not touch or handle the freight - unless you are negligent in your business operations concerning the shipment, or you have brought liability upon yourself.

Claim Forms

The principle purpose of the claim form is to notify the carrier and carrier's insurance of a damage or loss, in order for the claim filing process to begin. The claim form must include the load reference number, the ship date, the origin and destination points, a detailed statement explaining the amount claimed, and how the claimant arrived at the value or amount claimed. The statement should be as detailed as possible and explain the situation as clearly and fully as possible. Some clients have their own claim forms they want to use. Or, you can send them a blank claim form via fax or email.

What to do if you have a client claim that needs to be filed: You receive notice of a possible claim, from your client, the consignee, or the carrier. It looks like a claim situation. Call your customer, make sure that they are aware of the situation, and explain to them that you will be happy to assist them in resolving the insurance claim with the carrier's insurance provider. Send the customer a claim form if they don't have one. Have them send the completed claim form and information back to you for forwarding to the carrier.

Keep accurate and detailed notes on all correspondence between you, the carrier, and the shipper, with dates and who you talked to each time. The clearer documentation that you can get closer to the incident, the more accurate it tends to be. Send a claim acknowledgement to your client, along with a letter that you are doing all that you can to expedite their insurance claim. If it is a large claim, send a certified copy to the carrier's insurance provider, as well as a copy of the claim to the carrier. Call and check on the status of the claim once or twice weekly. The carrier or the carrier's insurance provider should send an acknowledgement of receipt for the claim within 30 days. When the settlement is sent to you, immediately send a check to your client with a resolution letter.

As a broker you should verify insurance on every load simply by calling the carrier's insurance company and asking if they are still covered. If you do this then you do not need any insurance.

Industry Standards

The shipper must tell you the value on every shipment so you can verify that the carrier's insurance company has the right amount of coverage for the load. In the expedited niche you will move freight that may be worth well over the limit of the carrier's insurance coverage.

Chapter
6

Goals, Plans & Practice

Do you currently have goals? Everybody has things they want to do. But have you really taken the time to think about them and plan how you are going to accomplish them? If not, you lower your chances of getting what you want. In fact, the rule is if you plan where you want to go, you'll probably get there; if you don't, you probably won't. Why are goals important? There are many things you can do with your time. Distractions are everywhere. This is especially true when you work out of your home. You can sleep late in the morning, go for a run, have extended lunches, watch television, and run errands, to name a few. The list is infinite. The best way to avoid the distractions is goal setting. It helps you to determine your priorities, to get organized, and to make decisions.

Seven Steps to Goal Setting

When you know what you want, and how to get there, it becomes easier to stay focused, not distracted. Here are seven steps that will help you to write goals that will keep you focused on being successful. 1. Make sure the goal you are working for is something you really want, not just something that sounds good. When setting goals it is also very important to remember that your goals must be consistent with your values. 2. A goal cannot contradict any of your other goals. For example, you can't buy a $75,000 car if your income goal is only $20,000 per year. This is called non-integrated thinking and will sabotage all of the hard work you put into your goals. 3. Develop goals in the various areas of your life. For example: Your Family and Home, Financial and Career, Spiritual and Ethical beliefs, Physical and Health areas, Social and Cultural, and Mental and Educational development. Setting goals in all areas of your life will ensure a more balanced life. 4. Be Positive! Work for what you want! Part of the reason why we write down and examine our goals is to create a set of instructions for our subconscious to carry out. Your subconscious mind is a very efficient tool, it cannot determine right from wrong and it does not judge. Its only function is to carry out its instructions. The more positive instructions you give it, the more positive results you will get. Thinking positively about the little things in everyday life will also help you in your growth as a human being. Don't limit it to goal setting. 5. Write your goals out in complete detail. Imagine your goals. Make it real in your mind's eye. 6. Make sure your goals are high enough. Shoot for the moon - if you miss you'll still be in the stars. Still in a great place. 7. Most importantly, write down your goals. Writing down your goals creates the road map to your success. Although just the act of writing them down can set the process in motion, it is also extremely important to review your goals frequently. Remember, the more focused you are on your goals the more likely you are to accomplish them.

Developing a Plan

Before you can reach any destination, you have to have a map and a plan. How are you going to get there? After you determine and write down your goals, it is important to break them down into achievable steps. Goals, by themselves, are not enough. The way to make a goal work is to sit down and make a plan. A goal, without a plan is just wishful thinking. You must have both. The goal is what. The plan is how.

Qualifying Potential Customers

This is very important! There are **five steps** in the process of qualifying potential customers.

Step 1 is the selection of prospects; those people who you believe will be interested in your services.

Step 2 requires that you call each of these prospects on the phone.

Step 3 demands that you establish your credibility. This is the beginning step. Establishing your credibility in the eyes of your customer is an on-going process from this point forward.

Step 4 is to develop a customer profile. You will be provided with a form that will provide the key pieces of information that you need. However, the information is not the only things you will need to learn about your customers. You have to be alert for the information that will help provide outstanding service, and will allow you to move the relationship forward.

Step 5 necessitates that you discover and confirm what the customer needs in terms of service from you. Only when you have moved to this point in the relationship will you be able to turn the prospect into a customer. Step two is to make the phone calls, all fifty of them. Develop the habit of writing down a daily call schedule. You don't have to make all 50 in one sitting. It might be easier, or fits into your schedule better, if you make the calls at two or three times during the day. What's important is to make ALL the calls. There are two types of calls that you will be making: Initial Contact Calls and Daily Calls.

Initial contact calls are made to establish contact and to qualify prospects. Daily calls are made to service customers. When you begin, most of your calls will be initial contacts. As you qualify prospects, the ratio of daily calls to initial calls will increase. You should keep the total number of calls at a minimum of 50 until you have a customer base that makes it impossible to make that number of calls. When you make contact with the prospect, you have 30 seconds or less, to gain their interest. Again, preparation is the key. Practice what you are going to say until you can say it without sounding like you are reading it, or making it up as you go along. Here's the process. Give them information about your company. (Why should they do business with you?) Pause and wait for their response. Answer any questions they might have. Ask, May I ask you some questions about your company? Move to step 4. Step 4 is to use the Client Profile to collect information about your client. There are four major areas where information must be gathered. Contact Information, Qualifying Information, Equipment/Service Requirements, and Competitive information. Starting from the first phone call, collect information for the profile. The best way to start is to ask for their permission. If they agree, then start asking questions. If they don't have time, ask for a specific time when it would be more convenient. If they are still reluctant, wait until your next call and try again.

Step 5 requires that you determine the needs of the prospect. What is important to this prospect? What are their expectations? How do they define service? Every client has different needs. Some care about problems being solved quickly. Some want fast service. Others care about how you treat their client. You must focus on their needs. Use open-ended questions to find out. Open-ended questions require more than a yes or no. They require the person asked to respond by disclosing needed information. For example, instead of saying, How many trucks do you send out each day?, you should ask, Could you tell me about your truck volume? With the open question, you will get more than the number of trucks. You may also learn about trends, strategies, the company's plans and other critical information. Use the customer profile as a guide of areas to explore. Expand your knowledge through open-ended questions. If you do all these things, THIS WILL WORK and YOU WILL BE **SUCCESSFUL!** Remember it takes hard work and dedication. I hope this helps provide insight on your future endeavor to become a freight broker or agent. Success to you!

Made in the USA
Middletown, DE
18 August 2020